Crock Pot Express Cookbook

Simple, Healthy, and Delicious Crock Pot Express Multi-Cooker Recipes For Everyone

Table of Contents

Introduction

Welcome to the Crock Pot Express Multi-Cooker Cookbook! You are about to get an in-depth look at the Crock Pot Express Multi Cooker and a wealth of simple, easy to make recipes. The recipes included will offer a variety of dishes that are great to eat and good for you.

Most of us have busy lives. Today's world demands this. Between work and family, many of us have trouble finding time to cook a decent, home-cooked meal. We often head out to a restaurant because it is faster and less stressful. However, restaurant food does not normally focus on healthy ingredients. This is the same for processed or premade foods, many carrying ingredients that are hard to pronounce or even know what they are.

I worked in a lot of restaurants when I was younger. From fast food to fine dining, I have seen them all. And no matter the "class" of restaurant, speed in preparation is important. As the years and technology have moved forward, many of the foods in restaurants are coming in pre-cooked, to simplify the process and get the food to you quickly. When it comes to knowing what goes into the food, most employees could not tell you easily. Yes, we are in a day and age where transparency has become important. However, you must remember that while you may get a calorie count and list of ingredients, ingredients allowed to go in foods is still very open.

Having this lack of control when eating out or buying processed, pre-made foods is frustrating. It forces us to make concessions on what we eat and provide for our families. Understand that I am a realist. I know that eliminating processed foods and minimizing eating out are both challenges. No matter who you are, you will still backslide. This is fine if most of the food being eaten by your family is under your control.

Home-cooked meals are ideal for a healthier lifestyle because you have control. You know what you want your family to eat, and can make sure they are getting the best food for their bodies. Also, home-cooked meals are often "comfort foods." All of us have some sort of comfort foods we love. Eating them usually reminds us of meals we ate at home as children. This is one of the joys of cooking at home; giving your children something to remember later in life, as they prepare these dishes for their family.

Cooking at home is also one of the best things for a family, as everyone sits around the table eating and talking. With the busy lives we all have, these opportunities should be created and cherished.

But, time is still the enemy isn't it? It robs us of opportunity when the pressure is on. That is why you need an option that allows you to create great meals that conform to your time constraints. Meals that rely on little preparation, and can cook without constant attention. This is where the Crock Pot Express Multi-Cooker comes in. It is a versatile cooker, that affords many ways to prepare a variety of meals and the means to control the time it takes.

Traditional crock pots require long cook times. Preparing a meal to cook all day is wonderful, but some days the morning rush is too much. Who has time to think about dinner when the kids cannot find their favorite shoes, or the dog needs to be walked? Fortunately, the Express Multi-Cooker can cook a great, healthy meal; in as little as an hour (you can breathe a little easier, and find those shoes). Plus, meals still taste great, like they have been simmering all day. This is versatility at its best.

I hope you enjoy this book and find it useful. I believe it will be a great way to enjoy cooking, save time and build some valuable family time and memories. Most of the recipes will be easy enough to allow anyone in the family to make a great meal.

Thank you again for choosing this cookbook. Have fun with it, and happy cooking!

What is the Crock Pot Express Multi-Cooker?

You have taken the first step to easier cooking by purchasing the Crock Pot Express Multi-Cooker. Now you want to know what it is, how it works and what it can do for you. No problem! Let's take a tour of the Express Multi-Cooker and see if we can broaden your horizons, and open your world to a wealth of cooking options from one appliance.

The Express Multi-Cooker is a one-stop, multi-faceted kitchen appliance. It can replace various appliances you may already have. It allows for easy preparation, simple setups and doesn't abuse your timetable. There are a wide range of recipes that can be prepared in the Multi-Cooker, which gets you away from cooking repetitive meals for convenience sake.

You will be able to prepare fresh meals, using fresh, wholesome ingredients that offer a healthy alternative to pre-packaged, processed foods. The best part is, foods cooked in the Multi-Cooker are more flavorful than traditional methods, as flavor is locked inside and infuses the food through the process.

From the technical side, the first thing to know about the Express Multi-Cooker is the available options for cooking. There are four primary functions:
- **Pressure Cooking** – Just like traditional pressure cookers, or the fast-cook method.
- **Slow Cooking** – Traditional multi-hour, slow-cook method.
- **Browning/Sauté** – Used for prepping meats or vegetables before slow or pressure cooking.
- **Steaming** – As implied, steams a variety of foods for lighter, low-fat dishes.

The Multi-Cooker also has eight pressure-cook settings for specific types of dishes. These settings will have your meals ready in a fraction of the time. These options are highly important when you need a great meal fast, because time was not available for slow cook setup early in the day.
- Meats/Stews
- Beans/Chili
- Rice/Risotto
- Poultry
- Soups
- Desserts
- Yogurt
- Multi-grains

It includes a large, dishwasher safe, 6-quart cooking pot, which is non-stick. The lid offers an airtight locking mechanism, the ability to delay cooking start times, and a setting for keeping food warm.

As you can see, that is a lot of versatility. On top of that, the Express offers a great display that informs you of cooking times, allows adjustments to cook times, shows temps and pressure, and indicator lights during the cooking process. It is very easy to use. So easy, you might find yourself using it to make most of your weekly meals.

There are a few things you should keep in mind when using the Multi-Cooker Express. Many of the functions you will be using have some general principles to keep in mind. Guidelines about the cooker and its functions will assist you in making great dishes.

Pressure Cooking Information

A key factor in using the Multi-Cooker, is understanding the pressure cooking features. High heat and pressure can lead to burns if not handled carefully. The cooker has features in place to avoid most issues.

For pressure to build in the Multi-Cooker:
- The lid must be shut properly.
- The Lid must be in the locked position.
- The Steam Release Valve must be in the Seal (sealed) position.

Functions using pressure cooking MUST have at least 8 ounces of liquid in the cook pot. You will know liquid is needed if an error message displays for pressure functions.

When pressure cooking has ended, the cooker will release pressure on its own. However, it does have a tab on the Steam Release Valve to manually release pressure. You must use a kitchen utensil when operating the tab on the Release Valve. After cooking has ended, give the cooker 10 minutes or so to release pressure naturally, then use the tab to ensure full release.

You can manually release pressure quickly using the Release Valve tab as well. Just remember not to do this in these instances:
- When cooking soups, stocks, casseroles or other "all-liquid" recipes.
- When cooking rice (can degrade stability of rice).

Note: If the lid is not opening, do not force. Pressure is preventing the lid from breaking its seal. Release the pressure manually, and wear an oven mitt when removing the lid.

Pressure cooking functions have two levels of pressure – LOW and HIGH.
- HIGH pressure works with many foods.
- LOW pressure is best for delicate foods like fish, vegetables and smaller size chicken pieces and fillets.

And don't forget, pressure needs to build, so watch for "HEAT" on the display when this is happening. Timers are not counting down while pressure builds.

Slow Cooker Functionality

Similar to pressure cooking functions, the Slow Cooker setting has HIGH and LOW settings. However, pressure is not used during cooking. HIGH and LOW refer to temperature levels. Basically, these settings are "basic" slow cooker settings. LOW being used for simmering and slowest cooking times, and HIGH for faster cooking in 1-4 hours.

Minor Pressure can still build in the unit in Slow Cooker mode, so make sure the Steam Release Valve is set to the Release position. This will limit pressure that builds and allow you to check and adjust food while cooking. To avoid steam burns, remember to lift the lid with an oven mitt on, like you would when pressure cooking.

Steam Cooker Functionality

The Steam function on the Multi-Cooker Express allows for general steaming of various foods. Steam cooking is a High Pressure function. Always use the same cautions as you would with pressure cooking. There is a steam rack to place food on, and liquid for steaming should be present, but not higher than the rack. You can refer to the user manual for cook time references for various foods.

Browning/Sautéing Functionality

This setting is easy to use and understand. It allows the cooker to act as a "sauté" skillet. This is a "dry" cook method, so no liquid is needed, though a lubricant can be used, i.e., butter, oil, etc. This is a great feature for searing meats to lock in flavor, or creating roux or mirepoix for thickening various recipes.

Bear in mind, you may want to cook in batches when using this function, due to size requirements. But, for many recipes, this eliminates the use of multiple pans during cooking. You can now brown or sauté right in the cook pot, and continue with your slow cook dish in the same cook pot.

Rice & Risotto Functionality

Just like it says, you can use your Multi-Cooker Express as a rice cooker. Rice is a great staple for many dishes. This function operates by using pressure, so follow guidelines referring to pressure cooking with this setting. Bear in mind that rice is going to expand, so avoid filling past the half-way mark while using this setting.

One thing to avoid when cooking rice is starch build up in the Steam Release Valve. The easiest way to avoid this, is proper washing of rice before cooking. Simply wash the measured rice in a strainer using cold water. When the water runs clear, excess starch has been cleaned from the rice. This excess starch is the culprit in build-up. The other advantage to washing rice, is a fluffier rice once cooking is done.

Specialty Functions

The food specific specialty settings on the Multi-Cooker Express allow you to fine tune cooking based off the dish. Remember, these settings will use pressure, except the YOGURT setting, and some afford the option of choosing LOW/HIGH for pressure levels. The manual has a guide that will allow you to determine cook times for these functions, based around the dish you are cooking.

The pressure cooking aspect requires the same cautions and guidelines as pressure cooking be used. Altitude/sea level can affect cooking with pressure, so adjust as needed if you live in extremely high or low sea levels.

Ultimately, become comfortable with these settings and the resulting cooking options. You will be able to cook these dishes much faster and more efficiently. The time savings afforded by these specialty settings is invaluable.

KEEP WARM Functionality

The KEEP WARM feature of the Multi-Cooker Express is one of my favorite features. Basically, when cooking completes, the cooker switches to KEEP WARM mode. This will let food finish and hold temperature for up to 4 hours after cooking ends. Now you don't have to worry that you missed the timer, or if someone is running a little late for dinner. This has always been a challenge with some slow cookers. For many, you must find some way to keep food from cooling too much when serving is not an option right away.

While this setting is not capable of cooking food, it can keep food warm enough to allow thickening agents to do their job. This is often a final step with soups and sauces. If the thickening requires higher heat, you will need to use the Slow Cooker setting, but some basic thickening can be accomplished with the KEEP WARM setting.

This is also my favorite setting for parties. I love making dips and other hot party snacks. You can cook these dishes in the Multi-Cooker Express and hold them in the fridge within the cook pot till party time. When near party time, simply pull the cook pot out, place in the cooker and use the Slow Cooker LOW setting 15-20 minutes to bring the temperature up. When the timer runs out, the unit will go into KEEP WARM mode and is ready for the party. You can set this up right on the serving table, and all you have to worry about is stirring the dish as it warms.

Final Advice: Cooking Tips

I would be remiss if I did not include some basic knowledge from the kitchen. Some of these tips may be old news for you, but bear with just the same.

The primary goal to cooking at home is making fresh meals that offer healthier benefits than processed foods from stores and restaurants. So, make sure to shop for the freshest ingredients you can. Some recipes are going to call for canned or pre-made products; however, if you want to invest a little time in making these ingredients yourself, please do. Sadly, not everyone can make a home-made version of creamed corn or tomato paste easily, so the pre-made version must suffice.

One ingredient that is often bought from the store is broth/stock (in case you aren't aware, broth and stock are essentially the same thing). Because there is a high level of sodium, and sometimes fat, in pre-made broths, it is best to make these from scratch. When cooking from scratch, you are in control of these levels. That is why there are recipes included for making your own stocks. I love to make stock and store in the freezer. The hold well for months, and are then readily available for use with just a little thawing.

However, you can still shop smart with these ingredients. Most products have a low-fat, low-sodium or fat-free option. These options should be explored. Just remember, some dishes require a certain level of "fats" for proper cooking; think cream based soups and sauces. The fats act as a smoothing and binding agent. It helps to remember that not all fats are bad, and moderation with fats is the key to success.

Fats are also important to remember when it comes to dairy in dishes. Some dishes that are not "fats" reliant allow for substitutions. If, for example, a dish does not offer the option to choose between 2%, 1% or fat-free milk, then it is recommended to not substitute the required milk. It helps to educate yourself on how fats work in cooking, if you don't already know.

When it comes to other substitutions, judgment must come in to play. Various herbs and spices are often interchangeable, as they are simply for flavor enhancement. Just bear in mind that certain herbs work well with certain meats. But, if you prefer to swap out herbs, you can. Use your best judgment and educate yourself on how these herb/spice changes will impact your dish.

If substituting major ingredients, like meat-free alternatives for making vegetarian versions of dishes, make sure you understand the stability of the substitute. Cooking times will have to be adjusted to avoid negatively impacting the food. If you are making an adjustment of this caliber, avoid using specialty functions, and opt for Slow Cooker functions. Since specialty functions are pressure based, you cannot physically monitor and control cooking adjustments. The Slow Cooker setting allows you to remove the lid and check the stability of the dish.

Being able to choose cooking alternatives requires a little homework on how to translate cook times from one setting to another. It is relatively easy to understand once you are comfortable with how LOW and HIGH pressures and temperatures work, and the times associated with them. Don't worry, it isn't rocket science, but once you know, you will be using each functionality for maximum benefit.

Finally, I will be honest, some recipes (primarily desserts) in this book are not as "health conscious" as one would hope. While this will require those with very specific diet requirements to substitute ingredients, for others, a little indulgence is okay. While everyone wants to eat healthy, remember the rule of moderation. Splurging in ones normally healthy diet will not destroy everything you are working for. In fact, occasional splurging with sweets, fats or carbohydrates can help you maintain a healthy diet. Odd to hear right?

The primary reason I say this is because diets restrict our thinking. When we are restricted in our thinking and allowances, we feel limited and often retract from our healthy approach. Remember, if you tell a child they cannot have a cookie, their next thought is how to get the cookie without alerting the authorities. You are human, so treat yourself sometimes. Exercise moderation. Exercise control. And, above all else, EXERCISE!

Controlled intake of food and calories, coupled with activity, keeps your metabolism on track, and calories burning.

The main thing to take away from cooking is pleasure. Whether it is the cooking process or eating the food itself, or both, cooking should be enjoyed. When you are making smart choices with ingredients and your diet, you will enjoy the food cooked even more. Using the Crock Pot Multi-Cooker Express is gives you so many great recipe choices, you will be hard pressed not to have fun.

Get your family involved, and teach them how to enjoy cooking as well. Family time in the kitchen is great for bonding and involvement. Food is a universal necessity for all of us. It binds us together as we sit and break bread together. Make the most of cooking, and make the most of your family, and friends, when it comes to cooking. Nothing beats a great meal, except sharing that meal with those we love. Enjoy!

Breakfast Recipes

Breakfast is always the most important meal for a successful start to your day. Remember, use long cook breakfast ideas for overnight cooking.

If making substitutions, keep cook times in mind, specifically if you are using meat alternatives. Turkey bacon requires different timing than pork bacon. In the vein of having fun with cooking, be creative and change things up when it comes to flavor additives like fruits. This will give dishes a new spin and keep your meal plan exciting for everyone.

DO NOT use the Delay Timer function with perishable ingredients; however, you can prep the night before and keep in fridge until ready to cook in the morning.

Now, on to the recipes!

Homemade Yogurt (with mixed berries)

Prep time: 5 minutes
Cook time: 8.5 hours (longer for tangier yogurt – shorter for less tangy yogurt)
Yield: ½ gallon

Ingredients:
- ½ gallon of milk (2%, 1% or fat free)
- 2 Tbsp. yogurt starter (yogurt made from active cultures and milk only)
- 1 cup mixed berries (suggested, can use 1 or more berries of choice)
- Cooking thermometer

NOTES: Make sure to chill the cooking pot before beginning. The YOGURT function cannot operate under pressure.

Instructions:
1. Add milk to cook pot.
2. Press YOGURT setting and set temperature to HIGH.
3. Set Steam Release Valve to the "Release" (open) position, and press START/STOP.
4. Whisk often. When cook cycle stops, check that temperature has reached 180°F.
5. Remove hot cook pot and place in cold water bath in sink. Do not get water in the cooking pot.
6. Cool milk to 95-105 degrees, whisking frequently. Do not add yogurt starter to hot milk to prevent killing bacterial cultures.
7. In a separate bowl mix milk from pot and yogurt starter together. Return mix to the cooking pot, stirring until mixture is of uniform consistency.
8. Place cooking pot back in heating base. Secure the lid. Ensure Steam Release Valve is still in open position. Press YOGURT, set temperature to LOW for 8-12 hours and press start.
9. Taste regularly after 8 hours until desired taste is reached. Once desired taste is achieved, press STOP. Remove Cooking Pot, cover with foil, and place in the fridge. This will end the incubating process.
10. Let yogurt cool for 8 hours. Yogurt will thicken while cooling.
11. Plain yogurt is done. Add berries of your choice and enjoy.

Fast Cook Oatmeal (with optional spices, nuts or fruits)

Pre time: 5 minutes
Cook time: 10 minutes
Yield: 3 serving

Ingredients:
- ½ cup cut oats
- 2 cups water
- 1 Tbsp. oil
- Dash of salt

Optional Add-Ins:
- ½ cup sliced strawberries
- ¼ cup sliced almonds
- 1 tsp. brown sugar

Instructions:
1. Combine oats, water, oil and salt in cook pot.
2. Secure the lid.
3. Press MULTIGRAIN setting. Set pressure to HIGH and set 10-minute cook time.
4. Set Steam Release Valve to the "Seal" (closed) position. Press START.
5. Once cook time finishes and pressure releases, remove yogurt from cook pot.
6. Top or mix in your choice of add-ins for preferred taste.
7. A variety of additions can be used. Choose fresh fruits or berries, assorted nuts and/or spices such as cinnamon, nutmeg, apple pie spice or more. This dish is great for seasonal variety.

Breakfast Apple cobbler

Prep time: 20 minutes
Cook time: 2 hours (short)/ 7-9 hours (long)
Yield: 4 Serving

Ingredients:

- 4 apples (medium), peel and slice to yield 2 cups
- ¼ cup honey
- 1 tsp. cinnamon
- 2 Tbsp. melted butter
- 2 cups granola cereal

Instructions:

1. Add apples in cook pot.
2. Mix in remaining ingredients.
3. Cover, set to Slow Cook LOW and cook 7-9 hours. (Can also be cooked on HIGH for 2 hours.)
4. Serve with cold milk.

Fruit and Nut Breakfast Casserole

Prep time: 10 minutes
Cook time: 3 hours
Yield: 4-6 serving

Ingredients:

- 3 Tbsp. melted butter
- 1 cup long cook oats
- 1 cup cream of wheat – uncooked
- 1 cup flour
- 1 cup brown sugar
- 1 egg, slightly beaten
- 1 cup milk
- ¼ cup oil
- 1 Tbsp. baking powder
- ½ tsp. salt
- 2 cups blueberries
- ¼ cup chopped walnuts

Instructions:

1. Mix all ingredients in separate bowl, except blueberries and nuts.
2. Once mixed, FOLD in nuts and blueberries.
3. Pour completed batter into cook pot.
4. Set cooker to LOW and cook for 3 hours or until casserole has set.
5. Serve warm with breakfast beverage of choice (cold milk suggested).

Creamy French Toast w/Bananas and Nuts

Prep time: 20 minutes
Cook time: 2-2.5 hours (fast)/ 3-4 hours (slow)
Yield: 10 slices

Ingredients:

- 1 (10-inch) French baguette (1-2 day old "stale" bread is best), cut into 1-inch slices
- 4 oz. cream cheese (room temperature)
- 3 to 4 bananas sliced
- 2 Tbsp. light brown sugar
- ½ cup chopped nuts (optional), walnut or pecan
- 3 eggs
- ¼ cup low-fat milk
- 1/3 cup honey
- 1 tsp. ground cinnamon
- Pinch of nutmeg
- ½ Tbsp. pure vanilla extract
- 2 Tbsp. butter cut into thin slices
- Honey, optional

Instructions:

1. Lightly grease cookpot with cooking spray.
2. Spread cream cheese on all bread slices (both sides) and arrange as a single layer on the bottom of the cook pot.
3. Layer banana slices on top of bread slices. Sprinkle with brown sugar. Add nuts if desired.
4. Placed sliced butter in layer over top. Set cook pot to the side.
5. In a mixing bowl, lightly beat eggs with whisk or beaters.
6. Add milk, nutmeg, cinnamon, honey and vanilla extract. Whisk or beat until thoroughly combined.
7. Pour mixture from bowl over bread.
   Do not let mixture cover the bread slices. Add liquid mixture until you reach ¾ of the way up solid layers.
8. Set cooker to LOW and cook 3 to 4 hours. Can be fast cooked on HIGH for 2 to 2.5 hours.
9. Remove lid. If not serving immediately, set cooker to warm and hold.
10. Serve with drizzled with honey. Add additional banana or nuts as topping if desired.

Crock Pot Cinnamon Rolls

Prep time: 25 minutes
Cook time: 90 minutes
Yield: 10 rolls

Ingredients:

For Dough:
- 2 cups self-rising flour
- 7 Tbsp. soft butter
- ½ tsp. salt
- ½ -1 cup milk
- ½ cup margarine (softened)

For Cinnamon Mix (combine following ingredients):
- 1 ¼ cups light brown sugar (packed)
- 2 ½ Tbsp. ground cinnamon
- 2 Tbsp. cornstarch

Instructions:

For Dough:
1. Combine flour, salt and butter in mixer.
2. Add milk slowly (as needed) to make dough.
3. Knead on floured surface. Roll out a rectangle measuring 20"x30".
4. Spread softened margarine on dough rectangle.

For Cinnamon Roll:
1. Cover dough with cinnamon mix. Using a rolling pin, press lightly into the dough.
2. Roll the dough tightly (20" length), then slice into 2" rolls.
3. Layer cook pot with parchment paper. Lay the rolls into the cook pot in single layer.
4. Use the MULTIGRAIN setting and cook for 90 minutes. Set Steam Release Valve to the "Seal" (closed) position. Press START.
5. Once cooking is complete, remove cinnamon rolls.
6. If desired, make a glaze with 1 cup powdered sugar and milk (add milk slowly until desired consistency reached). Drizzle glaze over rolls if desired.

Yummy Pecan Sticky Buns

Prep time: 30 minutes (additional 45 minutes for dough to rise)
Cook time: 60-75 minutes
Yield: 12 buns

Ingredients:

For Dough:
- 6 Tbsp. nonfat milk
- 4 Tbsp. maple syrup
- ½ Tbsp. unsalted butter, melted
- 1 tsp. vanilla extract
- ¼ tsp. salt
- 2 ¼ tsp. yeast
- 1 ½ – 2 cups whole wheat flour

For Caramel Sauce:
- 2 Tbsp. unsalted butter
- 2 Tbsp. nonfat milk
- 4 Tbsp. maple syrup
- ¼ cup chopped pecans

For Filling:
- 3 Tbsp. maple syrup
- 1 ½ tsp. ground cinnamon
- ½ Tbsp. unsalted butter, melted

Instructions:

For Dough:
1. Lightly coat cook pot with nonstick cooking spray. (clean residue from lid rim if present)
2. To prepare dough, combine milk, maple syrup, butter, and vanilla in a microwave-safe bowl.
3. Microwave for 20-second intervals on high. Stir for one minute after each interval, until butter has melted. The mixture should be warm, not hot (~110 degrees).
4. Add yeast and let it sit until frothy, 10-15 minutes.
5. Add flour, ½ cup at a time, until a dough forms and does not stick to the sides of mixer.

6. Place dough onto a well-floured surface, and knead until the dough springs back when gently pressed with a finger. Allow dough to rest while sauce and filling are prepared.

For Caramel Sauce and Filling:
1. For the caramel sauce, combine milk, butter, and syrup in the cook pot. Use the BROWN/SAUTÉ setting, and stir constantly until butter is melted. Continue stirring till sauce thickens and darkens slightly. Sprinkle the pecans on caramel sauce. Leave a ½" border around the edge.
2. For the filling, whisk together the maple syrup and cinnamon in a small bowl.

For Sticky Buns:
1. Roll dough out on floured surface to a 10"x14" rectangle.
2. Brush with the melted butter, then spread filling over buttered dough. Leave a ½" border on long edges. Roll dough into log (14"). Cut roll into 4 equal quarters, then slice each quarter into 3 slices. Layer on caramel sauce in cook pot.
3. Close the lid and set to WARM for approximately 45 minutes, or until rolls rise and double in size. Once risen, use Slow Cooker HIGH setting and cook for 60-75 minutes.
4. After rolls are cooked, allow to cool for 10-15 minutes, then place cooking rack or serving dish over cook pot and invert rolls onto rack/dish. Enjoy!

Southern Sausage and Biscuit Casserole w/Gravy

Prep time: 20 minutes
Cook time: 1-2 hours (depending on LOW or HIGH setting)
Yield: 6-8 serving

Ingredients:

- 1 lb. sausage
- 1 can biscuits
- 8 eggs
- 1 ½ cups cheddar cheese shredded
- 2 cups 2% milk
- ¼ cup melted butter
- ¼ cup all-purpose flour
- 1 tsp. salt
- 1 ½ tsp. ground black pepper

Instructions:

1. Using BROWN/SAUTÉ setting, brown sausage and drain well. Wipe excess grease from cook pot.
2. Coat inside of cook pot with cooking spray or with vegetable oil.
3. Combine eggs, sausage, and cheese in cookpot. Season with salt and pepper as you normally would.
4. Cut biscuits into small, bite-sized pieces. Place biscuits on top of the egg mixture.
5. Cook on Slow Cook HIGH for 1 hours, or on Slow Cook LOW for 2 hours.

For Gravy:

1. In small saucepan, whisk butter and flour together until it starts turning a golden brown. Add salt and pepper. Slowly stir in milk until all is incorporated. Continue stirring frequently over medium-high heat until gravy reaches a boil. Reduce heat and simmer 1-3 minutes until gravy thickens.
2. Serve casserole topped with gravy.

Southwest Style Breakfast Casserole

Prep time: 5-8 minutes
Cook time: 1-2 hours (dependent on LOW or HIGH setting)
Yield: 4-6

Ingredients:

- 20 oz. of frozen hash browns or 1.25 lbs. potatoes peeled and shredded
- 1 ½ cup diced ham
- 4 eggs
- ¼ cup milk
- 1 cup shredded pepper jack cheese (optionally use cheddar or Colby if desired)

Instructions:

1. Spray cook pot with cooking spray or wipe with oil.
2. Pour potatoes into cook pot and top with ham.
3. Whisk milk and eggs together. Pour over ham and potatoes.
4. Add shredded cheese on top of mixture.
5. Cook on Slow Cook LOW for 2 hours, or cook on HIGH for 1 hour.
6. Serve and enjoy!

Breakfast Burritos

Prep time: 5-15 minutes
Cook time: 1-2 hours (dependent on LOW or HIGH setting)
Yield: 6 serving

Ingredients:

- 12 eggs
- 2 cups diced red potatoes (substitute 20 oz. of frozen diced red potatoes)
- 1 cup 2% milk or almond milk (for dairy free)
- 1 cup diced ham
- Salt and pepper to taste

Instructions:

1. Spray cook pot with non-stick cooking spray or wipe with cooking oil.
2. Place the potatoes in the bottom of the cook pot and top with the diced ham.
3. Whisk together the eggs, milk, salt and pepper. Pour over the potatoes & ham.
4. Cover and cook on Slow Cook LOW for 2 hours or Slow Cook HIGH for 1 hour.
5. Roll 1 cup of cooked mix into large flour tortilla (substitute gluten-free tortillas if desired).
6. OPTIONAL: Add salsa, diced tomatoes, chives, shredded cheese, sour cream, or any other toppings you enjoy.

Veggie Omelet

Prep time: 15 minutes prep time
Cook time: approximately 1 hour
Yield: 8 serving

Ingredients:
- 6 eggs
- ½ cup milk
- ¼ tsp. salt
- Fresh ground pepper, to taste
- ¼ tsp. garlic powder, or to taste
- ¼ tsp. chili powder, or to taste
- 1 cup broccoli florets
- 1 red bell pepper, thinly sliced
- 1 small yellow onion, finely chopped
- 1 garlic clove, minced

Garnish:
- Shredded cheddar cheese
- Chopped tomatoes
- Chopped onions
- Fresh parsley

Instructions:
1. Coat the inside of the cook pot with cooking spray or oil; set aside.
2. Using a large mixing bowl, combine milk, eggs, pepper, salt, garlic powder and chili powder. Beat eggs with a whisk or beaters. Beat the mixture until combined well.
3. Add sliced peppers, broccoli, minced garlic and onions to the cook pot.
4. Pour in the egg-mixture.
5. Cover and set to Slow Cooker HIGH for 1 hours. Start checking at 30-45 minutes. Omelet is ready when eggs are set.
6. Sprinkle with shredded cheese and replace cover. Let omelet stand for 3 minutes or until cheese is melted.
7. Turn off cooker, cut omelet into 8 wedges and transfer to a serving plate.
8. Garnish with chopped onion, tomatoes and/or fresh parsley.
9. Serve and enjoy!

Three cheese shrimp and grits

Prep time: 10 minutes
Cook time: 1-3 hours (dependent on desired cook time)
Yield: 6 serving

Ingredients:
- 6 cups chicken stock
- 1 ½ cup quick cooking grits
- 1 Tbsp. garlic powder
- 1 Tbsp. onion powder
- 1 tsp. dried thyme or 2 tsp. fresh chopped thyme
- Salt and pepper, to taste
- 1 cup light sharp cheddar cheese
- 4 oz. light cream cheese
- ½ cup grated Parmesan, Romano or Asiago cheese (Reserve a bit for garnish)
- ½ tsp. hot sauce (optional)
- 2 lbs. raw shrimp (deveined if preferred)
- Scallions or chives and extra cheese for garnish
- ½ cup fat-free half and half (optional for "creamy" grits)

Instructions:
1. Combine chicken stock and grits in cook pot.
2. Add remaining ingredients EXCEPT shrimp and green onions.
3. Set to Slow Cooker LOW for 2 hours. For a faster cook time, use the RICE/RISOTTO setting with a 30-minute cook time. Make sure the Steam Release Valve is set to Sealed.
4. Once complete, add shrimp and half and half (if desired). If grits have absorbed all liquid, add some more stock.
5. Set to Slow Cooker HIGH and cook for 30 minutes, or until shrimp are done.
6. Serve with a garnish of shredded cheese and chives/scallions, as desired. Enjoy!

Banana Bread

Prep time: 10 minutes
Cook time: 1.5 hours
Yield: 2 servings

Ingredients:
- 2 eggs
- ½ cup butter (softened stick, or melted in microwave)
- 1 cup sugar
- 2 cups flour
- 1 tsp. baking powder
- ½ tsp. baking soda
- ½ tsp. salt
- ¼ tsp. ground cinnamon
- ¼ tsp. nutmeg
- 3 medium bananas, mashed
- ¾ cup sliced almonds (optional)

Instructions:
1. Prepare a loaf pan by coating with non-stick cooking spray, oil or butter.
2. In a bowl, stir together butter, sugar, and eggs, until well combined.
3. Add baking powder, baking soda, salt, cinnamon, and nutmeg to butter and sugar mixture.
4. Stir in flour. The mixture will be a little dry at this point.
5. Combine dough with mashed bananas and almonds, stir until well combined.
6. Pour mixture into loaf pan. Cover loaf pan with a paper towel and foil.
7. Add 1½ cups of water to the cook pot and insert the steam rack. Place the covered loaf pan on the steaming rack.
8. Using the MULTIGRAIN setting with High pressure, set a 1-hour timer. Ensure that the Steam Release Valve is set to Sealed.
9. When finished, the top should be slightly browned. A toothpick inserted in the middle should come out warm and clean.
10. Remove loaf from cooker and let cool. Once cool, separate bread from loaf pan with a butter knife inserted around the edge. Slice, serve and enjoy!

Apple Fritter Bread

Prep time: 1.5 hours (includes dough rising time)
Cook time: 1 hour
Yield: Varied based on portion size

Ingredients:

- 1 (0.25 oz.) pkg. active dry yeast {about 2¼ tsp.}
- 1 Tbsp. honey
- 1 ¼ cups warm water
- 1 ½ tsp. coarse salt
- 3 cups whole wheat pastry flour + a few spoonfuls
- 2 Tbsp. ground flax seed {optional}
- 2-3 medium sweet apples, diced
- ½ cup walnuts, chopped
- 2 Tbsp. butter, melted
- 1½ tsp. cinnamon
- 2 Tbsp. brown sugar

Instructions:

1. Place yeast, honey and warm water in stand mixer bowl. Use a whisk to combine ingredients. Let stand for 15-20 minutes, until mixture has puffed up.
2. Using mixer dough hook, run mixer at low speed. Add salt, then mix flour in ½ cup at a time. If flax seed is desired, add in as well.
3. Continue mixing on low speed for 4-5 minutes, until a ball has formed. Dough will be slightly sticky. Add in nuts and diced apples and mix until combined.
4. Dust a large piece of parchment paper with a few spoonfuls of flour. Remove dough from mixer, place on parchment and form a dough ball.
5. Using a damp cloth, cover the dough and allow it to rise for 1 hour or until it has doubled in size.
6. Place dough with parchment paper into a loaf pan.
7. Whisk melted butter, brown sugar and cinnamon together in a liquid measuring cup. Pour mixture over dough and swirl into the dough with a butter knife.
8. Cover loaf pan with a paper towel and foil.
9. Add 1½ cups of water to the cook pot and insert the steam rack. Place the covered loaf pan on the steaming rack.
10. Using the MULTIGRAIN setting with High pressure, set a 1-hour timer. Ensure that the Steam Release Valve is set to Sealed.

11. Once bread is complete, top should be browned. Let stand for 15-30 minutes to cool, then remove from loaf pan by running butter knife around edges to loosen. Flip out on to cutting board.
12. Slice and serve. Enjoy!
13. NOTE: Bread can be kept in the freezer for up to 30 days. Will hold for about 5 days in a sealed bag or container.

Basic Need Recipes

Many recipes may call for some basic needs, such as stocks. Here are some recipes to meet those needs. I will always recommend homemade stocks over store-bought broths. The are healthier and easy to make.

One tip for making stocks, save chicken and beef bones from previous meals. Store them in the freezer until you have enough to make stock. This way you limit the amount of ingredients to buy. This is why I will often buy boned chicken and debone myself, or cut beef or pork ribs from the bone before serving.

NOTE: Meat stocks can be frozen for up to 6 months if properly stored. Store in 1-2 cup amounts, or larger if desired, and thaw as needed for recipes.

Chicken Stock

Prep time: 20-30 minutes
Cook time: 1 hour
Yield: 1 gallon

Ingredients:

- 2 lbs. chicken carcass (bones and skin) from chicken (free-range preferred)
- 1 onion rough chopped (large chop is okay)
- 2 large carrots rough chopped (large chop is okay)
- 2 stalks of celery rough chopped (large chop is okay)
- ¼ cup fresh chopped parsley (or 2 Tbsp. dried parsley)
- 4 quarts water
- 2 tsp. salt
- 2 tsp. black peppercorns

Instructions:

1. Add chicken carcass, onion, carrots, celery and parsley to cook pot. Add salt and peppercorns.
2. Add water to Crock Pot.
3. Select SOUP setting and set time to 1 hour. Make sure Pressure Release Valve is in Seal position.
4. Once cooking is complete, let stock cool for 1 hour.
5. Place a drainer/colander in large bowl or pan. Pour chicken stock into colander. Remove the colander, which will separate all solids from the stock.
6. Stock is ready for use or for storing. Use freezer safe containers if you plan to freeze for future use. Make sure to use stock within six months of freezing.

NOTE: Chicken bones can be frozen and reused, but flavor quality diminishes with subsequent use.

Vegetable Stock

Prep time: 20 minutes
Cook time: 1 hour
Yield: 1 gallon

Ingredients:

- 1 large onion rough chopped
- 2 cloves crushed garlic (fresh garlic is best)
- 3 carrots rough chopped
- 4 stalks celery (including tops) rough chopped
- 1 bell pepper rough chopped
- 4 mushrooms chopped
- 1 Tbsp. olive oil
- 1 bay leaf
- 1 tsp. each (all or some): Parsley, rosemary, basil, oregano (if you have fresh herbs, use two sprigs of each, chopped)
- 4 quarts water
- 2 tsp. salt or 1 Tbsp. soy sauce

Instructions:

1. Add the onions, garlic, carrots, celery, bell pepper, and mushrooms to the cook pot.
2. Drizzle with olive oil and add in the bay leaf along with your herbs of choice.
3. Select SOUP setting and set time to 1 hour. Make sure Pressure Release Valve is in Seal position.
4. Once finished, stir in salt or soy sauce (whichever you choose).
5. Place a drainer/colander in large bowl or pan. Pour vegetable stock into colander. Remove the colander, which will separate all solids from the stock.
6. Stock is ready for use or for storing. Use freezer safe containers if you plan to freeze for future use. Make sure to use stock within six months of freezing.

Beef Stock

Prep time: 20-30 minutes
Cook time: 1 hour (dependent on temp selection)
Yield: 1 gallon

Ingredients:

- 3 lbs. beef bones (easy to get from local butcher/market, or store in freezer from previous meals) **NOTE: Pork ribs can be used if needed, just add a beef bullion cube to the stock while cooking.**
- 2 medium onions rough chopped (large chop is okay)
- 2 large carrots rough chopped (large chop is okay)
- ¼ cup fresh chopped parsley (or 2 Tbsp. dried parsley)
- 2 sprigs fresh rosemary (2 tsp. dried)
- 8 fresh basil leaves chopped (1Tbsp. dried)
- 4 quarts water
- 2 tsp. salt
- 2 tsp. black peppercorns

Instructions:

1. Add beef bones, onion, carrots and herbs to cook pot. Add salt and peppercorns.
2. Add water to Crock Pot.
3. Select SOUP setting and set time to 1 hour. Make sure Pressure Release Valve is in Seal position.
4. Once cooking is complete, let stock cool for 1 hour.
5. Place a drainer/colander in large bowl or pan. Pour beef stock into colander. Remove the colander, which will separate all solids from the stock.
6. Stock is ready for use or for storing. Use freezer safe containers if you plan to freeze for future use. Make sure to use stock within six months of freezing.
7. NOTE: Beef bones can be frozen and reused, but flavor quality diminishes with subsequent use.

Soups

Not many foods can offer the comfort of a great soup. Soups are great during cold weather or when you are not feeling well. Soups are even great during warm weather months on occasion. Many soups can be frozen for a short while, so feel free to store them. Just make sure to check how long you can freeze them safely.

With soups, fats can be important. This means exercise care when making substitutions, so you don't hurt the stability of your dish. Also, use care when adjusting cooking times or temperatures. Soups, especially those with cream/dairy, can be temperamental. If temperatures run too high, the soup will "break" or separate; basically, the fat separates from the liquids. Broken soups can be next to impossible to fix without messing up the taste or stability of the soup.

Have fun with soups. They are a comfort dish your family will enjoy every time.

Potato Soup

Prep time: 20 minutes
Cook time: 1 hour (fast)/ 6-8 hours (slow)
Yield: 6-8 serving

Ingredients:

- 6 cups of peeled potatoes (slice or dice)
- 8 oz. sliced mushrooms
- 2 bags "real" bacon bits
- 2 cans low-fat cream soup (mushroom or celery)
- 3 cups of whole milk (2% can be substituted)
- 1 cup diced onions (optional)
- 1-3 tsp. minced garlic (optional)
- Shredded cheese (optional)

Instructions:

1. Spray cook pot with non-stick cooking spray or wipe down with olive oil (preferred).
2. Open all your cans but do not drain them.
3. Use a potato masher and mash up to half the potatoes.
4. Pour all the ingredients into cook pot. Stir well.
5. Use the Slow Cook setting on LOW for a long cook of 6-8 hours. For quicker results, select SOUP setting and adjust time to 60 minutes. Ensure Pressure Valve is in Sealed position and Start.

Taco Soup

Prep time: 15 minutes (30 minutes for chicken)
Cook time: 1 hour
Yield: 6-8 serving

Ingredients:

- 1 (16 oz.) can pinto beans
- 1 (16 oz.) can white beans or 1 (16 oz.) can kidney beans
- 1 (11 oz.) corn
- 1 (11 oz.) can Rotel tomatoes & chilies
- 1 (28 oz.) can diced tomatoes
- 1 (4 oz.) can diced green chilies
- 1 (1 ¼ oz.) envelope taco seasoning mix
- 1 (1 oz.) envelope Hidden Valley® Original Ranch® Dressing and Seasoning Mix
- 1 lb. lean ground beef or shredded chicken.

Instructions:

1. Using the SAUTÉ setting, cook beef and drain. If using chicken, broil in oven then shred.
2. Open cans but do not drain liquid. Add all ingredients (with liquid) to cook pot. Stir together well.
3. Select SOUP setting, set time to 1 hour and make sure Steam Release Valve is Sealed.
4. Once complete, leave KEEP WARM on until time to serve.
5. Garnish with sour cream, shredded cheese, chopped green onions, or tortilla chips.

Vegetable soup

Prep time: 10 minutes
Cook time: 1 hour (6 hours for slow cook)
Yield: 8-10 serving

Ingredients:

- 2 (14 oz.) cans of diced tomatoes un-drained
- 1 large onion chopped
- 4 garlic cloves (pressed or minced)
- 2 Tbsp. olive oil divided
- 2 large carrots chopped
- 2 stalks of celery chopped
- 2 cups green beans cut in 1-inch pieces (can substitute one 14 oz. can of cut beans, drained)
- 6 cups of chicken or vegetable stock
- ¼ head of cabbage chopped
- ½ tsp. thyme
- 1 tsp. salt
- ½ tsp. pepper (black or white)
- 2 small russet potatoes (peeled and diced)

Instructions:

1. Using the BROWN/SAUTÉ setting, add one tablespoon of olive oil and onion. Sauté onion until "transparent."
2. Add garlic to onion sauté. Do not let the garlic brown, and sauté another couple of minutes.
3. Add all the chopped vegetables. Use the additional tablespoon of olive oil as needed to assist sauté. Sauté for up to two minutes. Do not cook vegetables fully, this is just to initiate flavor release. While sautéing, add the thyme, salt and pepper.
4. Once sauté is complete, add chicken stock and diced tomatoes. Stir well.
5. You can use Slow Cook LOW for a 6-hour long cook. For faster preparation, select the SOUP setting, set time to 1 hour, ensure the Steam Release Valve is in Seal position, then Start.
6. Once soup is finished, you can mash some of the potatoes and stir to thicken broth slightly, if preferred.
7. This soup serves well with grilled cheese sandwiches.

Variations:

- **Tex Mex** – Use black beans instead of green beans and cabbage. Add 3-4 sprigs of fresh cilantro (chopped). Add ½ tsp. cumin. Top served soup with shredded cheese and tortilla chips.
- **Tuscan Veggie** – Replace green beans with white kidney beans (drained and rinsed). Replace cabbage with chopped kale. Add 1 Tbsp. Italian seasoning.
- **Autumn Veggie** - Add 2 cups diced acorn squash or butternut squash. 1 cup cooked brown rice. ½ tsp. of nutmeg, and ¼ fresh parsley, chopped.

Detox Vegetable Soup

Prep time: 15 minutes
Cook time: 1.5 hours (7 hours for slow cook)
Yield: 6-8 serving

Ingredients:
- 2 cloves garlic crushed
- 1 medium onion roughly chopped
- 3-4 cups kale roughly chopped
- 2 medium carrots peeled and roughly chopped
- 1 large zucchini roughly chopped
- 1 1/2 cup green beans chopped bite size
- 14 oz. can diced tomatoes
- 1 qt. vegetable broth
- 1 Tbsp. balsamic vinegar (or juice of 1 lemon juice)
- 1 tsp. salt
- ½ tsp. pepper

Instructions:
1. Add all ingredients EXCEPT zucchini and balsamic vinegar (or lemon juice) to the cook pot.
2. You can use Slow Cooker LOW for 6 hours for long cook time. When cooking is complete, add zucchini and cook on LOW for 1 more hour.
3. For faster cooking, use SOUP setting with a 30-minute cook time, making sure the Steam Pressure Valve is set to Sealed. Once finished and pressure has released, add zucchini and cook on Slow Cooker LOW for 1 more hour.
4. After final cook with zucchini, add balsamic vinegar (or lemon juice), salt and pepper. Serve and enjoy!

Hamburger Soup

Prep time: 15-20 minutes (includes cooking pasta)
Cook time: 1-4 hours (depending on desired timing)
Yield: 6 serving

Ingredients:

- 1.5 lbs. extra-lean ground beef
- 1 whole onion, diced
- 4 whole carrots, peeled and sliced
- 4 stalks celery, sliced
- 10.75 oz. tomatoes (canned diced, with green chilis such as Rotel brand)
- 6 oz. tomato paste
- 2 Tbsp. beef base
- 2 tsp. dried oregano
- 1 Tbsp. salt
- 2 tsp. black pepper, freshly ground
- 1 Tbsp. garlic powder
- 3 cloves garlic, minced
- 2 Tbsp. Worcestershire sauce
- 2 cups water
- 8 oz. pasta (rotini or penne suggested)

Instructions:

1. Use the BROWN/SAUTÉ setting and brown ground beef. Drain well.
2. Add remaining ingredients EXCEPT pasta into cook pot.
3. You can choose a long cook time by using Slow Cooker HIGH for 4 hours. For a faster cook time, use the SOUP setting with a 1-hour time setting. Make sure Steam Release Valve is set to Sealed.
4. Cook pasta in separate pot. Serve pasta in bowl with soup ladled in. Enjoy!

Chicken Noodle Soup

Prep time: 20 minutes prep time
Cook time: 1.25-4.25 hours (dependent on preferred cook timing)
Yield: 8-10 serving

Ingredients:
- 3 carrots peeled, then chop or slice
- 3 celery stalks chopped
- 1 large onion chopped
- 3 boneless skinless chicken breast halves cut into bite-size chunks
- 32 oz. of chicken stock (use 2 16 oz. cans of fat-free chicken broth if desired)
- 6 cups of water
- 1 tsp. dill (fresh preferred)
- 2 sprigs fresh parsley chopped (1 Tbsp. dried parsley if preferred)
- 8 oz. egg noodles (recommend no-yolk variety)

Instructions:
1. Add vegetables, chicken, chicken stock and water to cook pot. Add dill and parsley and stir well.
2. For long cook, use Slow Cooker HIGH with a 4-hour timer.
3. For fast cooking, use the SOUP setting with a 1-hour timer. Make sure Steam Release Valve is set to Sealed.
4. Once cooking is complete, add noodles. Use the Warm setting for 15-25 minutes to allow noodles to cook. Check noodles for doneness at 15 minutes, and turn off heat as soon as noodles are tender.

Cheddar Broccoli Soup

Prep time: 20 minutes
Cook time: 1-3 hours (dependent on desired timing)
Yield: 8-10 serving

Ingredients:

- 6 Tbsp. butter
- 1 onion chopped
- 2 lbs. chopped broccoli (frozen broccoli can be substituted)
- 8 cups of chicken stock (fat-free chicken broth if stock not available)
- 16 oz. fat-free Velveeta, cubed
- 16 oz. shredded low-fat, sharp cheddar cheese
- 2 cups half and half
- 4 cloves garlic minced
- 2/3 cup of cornstarch
- 1 cup water

Instructions:

1. Using BROWN/SAUTÉ setting, add Velveeta and half & half. Cook until melted, stirring frequently. Once melted, stir in chicken stock and let heat. Do not let liquid boil.
2. While melting cheese, place cornstarch in bowl. Slowly stir in water a few Tbsp. at a time to avoid clumping, and create a slurry. Add water until finished and slurry is smooth.
3. Slowly add some melted cheese sauce to slurry to temper. When slurry is warm, add to the cheese sauce in cook pot.
4. Stir in remaining ingredients EXCEPT shredded cheese.
5. For a long cook time, use Slow Cooker HIGH with a 3-hour timer.
6. For faster cook time use the SOUP setting with a 45-minute timer. Make sure Steam Release Valve is set to Sealed.
7. Once cooking is complete, set to WARM for 15 minutes and stir in shredded sharp cheddar.
8. Should soup be thicker than desired, add water in slowly (1 Tbsp. at a time) until desired consistency is achieved.
9. Serve with warm, crusty bread, or in a bread bowl. Enjoy!

Turkey Soup

Prep time: 15 minutes
Cook time: 1.5-4.5 hours (based on timing preference)
Yield: 6-8 servings

Ingredients:
- 4 cups turkey stock (4 cans of turkey broth can be substituted)
- 2 cups diced cooked turkey
- ¼ Vidalia onion, chopped
- 1 cup celery, diced
- 1 cup carrot, diced
- ½ tsp. dried basil
- ¼ tsp. dried thyme
- 2 cups diced potatoes
- ½ cup 2% low-fat milk
- ½ cup cream
- ½ up flour

Instructions:
1. Add turkey, vegetables and herbs to cook pot.
2. Add turkey stock until it just covers meat and veggies.
3. For slow cook, use Slow Cooker HIGH with a 4-hour timer.
4. For fast cook, use the SOUP setting with a 1-hour timer.
5. Mix milk, cream and flour in a bowl, then add to soup, stirring well.
6. Set to Slow Cooker LOW and cook for 30 more minutes, stirring every few minutes until thickened. You can stop cooking when soup reaches desired consistency.

Meat Dishes (Beef/Pork/Lamb)

Meats are a long time favorite dish for many people. The variety of dishes that meat affords is amazing. Nearly every culture has dishes that use meat to its best advantage. There are many schools of thought on meat and its health advantages or disadvantages. However, like anything else, moderation is key.

When preparing meat dishes, you can substitute one meat for another to try new options. If you do, make sure you do the homework and make smart time and temperature adjustments. If using non-meat alternatives, this is crucial.

Also, many beef and pork dishes work well with poultry as a substitute. Again, this is great for diversity, but requires you make those smart choices in cooking methods.

Steak Fajitas

Prep time: 15 minutes
Cook time: 3 hours
Yield: 6-8 serving

Ingredients:
- 1 ½ lbs. boneless sirloin, cut into thin strips
- 2 Tbsp. olive oil
- 2 Tbsp. lemon juice
- 1-2 garlic clove, minced
- 1 ½ tsp. ground cumin
- 1 tsp. seasoning salt
- ½ tsp. chili powder
- 1 green bell pepper, thinly sliced
- 1 onion, thinly sliced
- 6 -8 flour tortillas

Toppings (Optional):
- Shredded cheddar cheese
- Salsa
- Guacamole
- Sour cream
- Shredded lettuce
- Chopped tomato
- Chopped onion

Instructions:
1. Using the BROWN/SAUTÉ setting, add olive oil and sirloin to cook pot and brown.
2. Add lemon juice, garlic, cumin, salt, and chili powder. Mix well.
3. Cover and cook on Slow Cooker HIGH for 2 hours, until meat is tender. When 2 hours is complete, add in green pepper and onion and cook for 1 more hour.
4. Warm the tortillas.
5. Spoon beef and veggies onto tortillas.
6. Top with cheese, salsa, sour cream, lettuce, and/or tomatoes if desired.
7. Fold tortillas around mix and toppings, then serve.

Pulled Pork

Prep time: 5-10 minutes
Cook time: 5-7 hours
Yield: Varies by portion/sandwich size

Ingredients:
- 4 lbs. pork roast (shoulder or butt)
- 2 large onions sliced
- 1 cup ginger ale
- 1 (18 oz.) bottle of your favorite barbecue sauce

Instructions:
1. Add half of the sliced onion to the cook pot.
2. Place roast over onion and cover with the rest of the onion.
3. Pour the ginger ale over the roast and onions.
4. Cover and cook on Slow Cooker LOW for 8-10 hours. Test meat at 8 hours to see if it pulls apart easily with a fork.
5. Alternatively, you can use Slow Cooker HIGH for 4-6 hours, checking meat for tenderness at 4 hours.
6. When done, remove the roast and place on pan for shredding. Strain onions from liquid and return to cook pot. Discard liquid. Using two forks, shred the meat. Discard any fat. Most of the fat will have rendered.
7. Add shredded meat to onions in cook pot and stir in the barbecue sauce.
8. Cover and cook on Slow Cooker LOW for 1 more hour.
9. Make sandwiches with hamburger buns, or your bread of choice. Use additional barbeque sauce as needed.
10. Pulled pork can be kept frozen for up to 30 days, if properly sealed and protected. You can also pre-make sandwiches and freeze, but ensure they are well protected (wrapped and bagged).
11. While other cuts can be used, the shoulder or butt shred best once cooked. Do not worry about increased fat content in these cuts, as the bulk of the fat will render away, and be discarded with liquid. The fat also does wonders for flavoring the meat.
12. You can turn the roast over during cooking if you prefer, to even out cooking. Use caution when turning the roast, as it will be unwieldy (recommend large serving forks), and liquids can splash.

Variation: For a slightly different flavor, instead of ginger ale, use a can of Diet Coke.

Teriyaki Beef

Prep time: 10-15 minutes
Cook time: 1.5-4.5 hours (dependent on desired timing)
Yield: 6-8 serving

Ingredients:

- 1 ½ lb. lean beef, cut in 1-inch cubes
- 1 (8 oz.) can crushed pineapple in juice, do not drain
- ½ cup water
- ½ cup low sodium soy sauce
- ¼ cup brown sugar
- ¼ tsp. ground ginger
- ¼ tsp. garlic powder
- 1 Tbsp. cornstarch
- White rice or brown rice, cooked

Instructions:

1. Add the pineapple with juice, water, soy sauce, sugar, & spices to a cook pot.
2. Using the BROWN/SAUTÉ setting, stir to melt the sugar then add in the beef cubes.
3. Cover with a lid then set to Slow Cooker HIGH with a 4-hour timer. Alternatively, you can use the MEAT setting with a 1-hour timer, ensuring that the Steam Release Valve is set to Sealed.
4. Once cooking has finished, mix the cornstarch with 2 Tbsp. of warm water, then stir into the sauce.
5. Re-cover & cook for another 20-30 minutes on Slow Cooker HIGH, until the sauce thickens. Do not use the MEAT setting for this finishing time.
6. Serve over rice and enjoy!

Citrus Herb Lamb Shanks

Prep time: 15 minutes
Cook time: 30 minutes
Yield: 4 serving

Ingredients:
- 4 lamb shanks
- ¼ cup olive oil
- ¼ cup flour
- 2 cloves crushed garlic
- 2 onions, chopped
- ¾ cup chicken stock
- 4 fresh dill sprigs
- 1 lemon, finely sliced
- 2 Tbsp. lemon juice
- ¼ tsp. salt
- ¼ tsp. ground black pepper
- Fresh dill, for garnish

Instructions:
1. Coat lamb with flour. Using the BROWN/SAUTÉ setting, add half of the olive oil and allow to preheat. Brown lamb shanks until they are golden brown; 3-5 minutes.
2. Remove shanks from cooker. Add second half of the olive oil, onion and garlic. Sauté until tender; 3-5 minutes.
3. After onion and garlic are tender, add lamb, dill, lemon slices and juice, and chicken stock to cook pot. Close and set the Steam Release Valve to Sealed. Use the MEAT setting with HIGH pressure and a 30-minute cook time.
4. When lamb has finished cooking, salt and pepper to taste. Use fresh dill for garnish, serve and enjoy.

Marinara w/Meatballs

Prep time: 20-25 minutes
Cook time: 2 hours
Yield: 6-8 serving

Ingredients:

- 2 Tbsp. of chopped fresh parsley
- 1 ¼ lb. extra lean ground beef
- 1/3 cup bread crumbs
- 2 Tbsp. grated Parmesan cheese
- 1 egg
- 1 clove garlic, minced
- 1 tsp. dried oregano
- ½ tsp. each salt and pepper
- 1 Tbsp. olive oil
- 1 lb. spaghetti, cooked according to package directions
- 1/3 cup shaved Parmesan cheese, to serve

For Marinara sauce:

- 1 Tbsp. olive oil
- 1 onion, chopped
- 2 cloves garlic, sliced
- Pinch hot pepper flakes
- ¼ cup tomato paste
- 1 can (28 oz.) diced tomatoes
- ¼ cup chopped fresh basil

Instructions:

1. In a large bowl, mix ground beef, cheese, egg, bread crumbs, oregano, garlic, parsley, salt and pepper until combined well. Then roll into 1" balls; target 24 meatballs.
2. Using the BROWN/SAUTÉ setting on HIGH. Add a Tbsp. of olive oil and begin browning the meatballs. You will need to cook in batches to prevent sticking together, burning or steam build up; space meatballs in cook pot while browning. Transfer meatballs to a plate or cookie sheet once browned, until ready to use.

For Marinara Sauce:

3. Once the meatballs are finished, continue using the BROWN/SAUTÉ setting for preparing the marinara.

4. Add a Tbsp. of olive oil, garlic, onion and the pepper flakes to the cook pot. Sauté for approximately 5-8 minutes, or until onion and garlic are softened/transparent.

5. Stir in the diced tomatoes and paste. Mix well and make sure any browned sauce at edges is incorporated as well.

6. Add in meatballs and close the lid. Use the Slow Cooker setting on LOW with a 2-hour timer. Make sure the Steam Release Valve is in the Release position.

7. Once done, serve sauce over your favorite pasta and garnish with Parmesan cheese. Enjoy!

Homestyle Beef Stew

Prep time: 15-20 minutes
Cook time: 2 hours
Yield: 6+ servings, based on portion size

Ingredients:
- 1 Tbsp. olive oil
- 1½ lb. stewing beef
- ½ tsp. each salt and pepper
- 2 cloves garlic, minced
- 2 tsp. finely chopped fresh thyme
- 2 Tbsp. tomato paste
- 1 ½ cups diced carrots
- 2 cups quartered baby red potatoes
- 1 cup pearl onions, peeled
- ½ cup red wine
- 2 cups beef stock
- 2 bay leaves
- 3 Tbsp. all-purpose flour
- 1 cup frozen peas, thawed
- 2 Tbsp. chopped fresh chives

Instructions:
1. Use the BROWN/SAUTÉ setting at HIGH temp. Once heated, add olive oil to the cook pot. Season beef with the salt and pepper, then add to cook pot. Cook the beef until well browned; approximately 6 or 7 minutes. Add the thyme and garlic and cook for another minute, stirring constantly.
2. Mix in the tomato paste, then the carrots, onions and potatoes.
3. Using a whisk, add the wine and beef stock, then drop in the bay leaves. Allow mixture to come to a boil.
4. Once done, close the cook pot and set to Slow Cook HIGH, with a 2-hour timer. Make sure the Steam Release Valve is set to the Release position. Check the stew during the final half of cooking to determine when vegetables and beef are tender. About 30 minutes before cooking finishes, you will need to make the thickening agent (next step).
5. Use a medium bowl and whisk the flour with a half cup of the cooked liquid. Once it is well mixed, add to the stew in cook pot, and stir well. Continue slow cooking for the last half hour, or until stew has thickened to desired consistency. Once done, add in the chives and peas. Also, before serving, remove the bay leaves from the stew.

Creamy Beef Stroganoff

Prep time: 15-20 minutes
Cook time: 4 hours
Yield: 6-8 serving

Ingredients:
- 2 Tbsp. olive oil
- ½ lb. sliced cremini mushroom
- 1 large onion, thinly sliced
- 1½ lb. beef sirloin steak, cut into ¼-inch slices
- ½ tsp. each salt and pepper
- 2 cloves garlic, minced
- 1 Tbsp. paprika
- ¼ cup tomato paste
- 1½ cups low-sodium beef stock
- 1 Tbsp. all-purpose flour
- 1 Tbsp. Worcestershire sauce
- 2 bay leaves
- ⅓ cup sour cream
- ¼ cup chopped fresh parsley
- 12 oz. egg noodles, cooked according to package directions

Instructions:
1. Use the BROWN/SAUTÉ setting on HIGH. Once heated, add half the olive oil to the cook pot. Next, add the onion and mushrooms. Cook, stirring constantly for approximately 5 minutes. Cook until browned lightly, then remove from cook pot and set to the side.
2. Place the remaining olive oil in the cook pot. Salt and pepper the beef, add to the cook pot and brown. Stir frequently; browning should take about 5 minutes. Remove from cook pot when done and set to the side.
3. Add garlic and paprika to the cook pot and return the mushrooms and onions. Stir in the tomato paste next and cook for about 1 minute.
4. Using a separate bowl, whisk together ¼ cup beef stock and the flour, then set to the side.
5. Pour the remaining beef stock into the cook pot, stirring to mix well. Next add Worcestershire and bay leaves. Add the browned beef back to the cook pot, then mix in the stock/flour thickening agent.
6. Close the lid. Use the Slow Cooker LOW setting with a 4-hour timer. Make sure the Steam Release Valve is set to Release.
7. Serve over the egg noodles you pre-cooked and enjoy.

Stuffed Peppers Enchilada Style

Prep time: 15 minutes
Cook time: 15 minutes
Yield: 5 serving

Ingredients:
- 5 bell peppers (any color)
- 1 ½ lb. ground beef
- 1 15oz can black beans, drained and rinsed
- 2 cups shredded pepper-jack cheese
- 1 can of corn, drained
- 1 small onion, diced
- ½ cup diced tomatoes
- 10 oz. can enchilada sauce
- 1 cup white wine
- 1 tsp. of cumin
- 1 tsp. garlic powder
- 1 tsp. salt
- 1 Tbsp. olive oil
- 1 jalapeño pepper, sliced (optional)
- 1 cup sour cream (optional)

Instructions:
1. Prepare the bell peppers by cutting the tops off and hollowing out. Remove all seeds and trim the white ribs, then discard. Set peppers aside.
2. Use the BROWN/SAUTÉ setting on HIGH. When heated, add olive oil and beef to the cook pot. Brown the beef for up to 5 minutes, being sure not to overcook. When done, drain the beef. Place the beef into a large mixing bowl.
3. In the mixing bowl, mix in the corn, cheese, black beans, onion, tomatoes, cumin, enchilada sauce, salt and garlic powder. Stir all ingredients until combined well. Next, stuff each pepper with the mixture.
4. Place the steaming rack in the cook pot, then add the wine. Set the stuffed peppers on the rack.
5. Close the lid. Use the BEANS/CHILI setting on LOW and set the timer to 15 minutes. Ensure that the Steam Release Valve is in the Sealed position and start cooking.
6. Once cooking is complete, garnish peppers with sour cream and/or jalapeño if you choose, then serve.
7. Note: If any stuffing mixture was left over, save for another recipe or make extra stuffed peppers.

"Stout" Corned Beef w/Vegetables

Prep time: 15-20 minutes
Cook time: 1.5-8 hours (dependent on timing preference – High or Low)
Yield: 8 serving

Ingredients:

- 4 lbs. corned beef brisket with seasoning pack provided
- 6 red potatoes, washed and cut into large chunks
- 1 lb. baby carrots
- 1 head of cabbage, sliced into sections ½" wide
- 1 can (15 oz.) of Guinness Stout (substitute dark, stout ale of choice if preferred)
- 3 cloves garlic, minced
- 2 Tbsp. sugar
- 2 Tbsp. apple cider vinegar
- ¼ tsp. ground black pepper

Instructions:

1. In order, layer the potatoes, carrots and cabbage in the cook pot. Pour in the Stout, apple cider vinegar, garlic, pepper and sugar over the vegetables. Rub the brisket with the provided seasoning packet. Place the brisket in the cook pot on the cabbage and close the lid.
2. Use the Slow Cooker LOW setting with an 8-hour timer. Make sure the Steam Release Valve is in the Release position before you start cooking. Once the brisket is finished, serve hot with vegetables as side dish.

Alternate Fast Cook Method:

Use the MEAT/STEW setting on HIGH with a 1.5-hour timer. Check that the Steam Release Valve is set to the Sealed position and start cooking. Once the brisket is finished, serve hot with vegetables as side dish.

Spaghetti Bolognese w/Spaghetti Squash

Prep time: 15-20 minutes
Cook time: 15 minutes – 8 hours (depending on desired timing – High or Low)
Yield: 4-5 serving

Ingredients:
- 1 large (approx. 3 lbs.) spaghetti squash
- 1 lb. ground beef
- 1 small onion, diced
- 3 cloves of garlic, minced
- 1 tsp. salt
- 1 tsp. black pepper
- 1 can (28 oz.) tomato sauce
- 1 cup beef broth
- 1 bay leaf
- 1 Tbsp. olive oil
- ¼ cup grated pecorino Romano cheese

Instructions:
1. Using the BROWN/SAUTÉ setting on HIGH. Once hot, add olive oil to the cook pot and brown the ground beef for 5 minutes; avoid overcooking.
2. Add in the onions and sauté for about two more minutes till onions are becoming tender. Next add in garlic, salt and pepper.
3. Stir in beef stock, tomato sauce and the bay leaf. Stir until well combined.
4. Next, poke holes in the squash with a large kitchen knife and set the whole squash in the cook pot over the sauce. If you prefer, use the steam rack for stability. Close the lid.
5. Use the Slow Cooker HIGH setting with a 6-8-hour timer. Check that the Steam Release Valve is in the Release position. At 6 hours, begin checking if the squash is tender by trying to pierce it with a fork.

Alternative Fast Cook Method:
1. Use the BEANS/CHILI setting on HIGH with a 15-minute timer. Ensure the Steam Release Valve is in the Sealed position before starting cook cycle.
2. Once cooking is done, and pressure has been released, check that squash can be pierced with a fork. Remove squash from the cook pot, and cut in half. Scrap out the seeds and throw away. Using a fork, remove the flesh from the squash. This should come out in long strands that look like spaghetti.

3. Serve meat from squash like spaghetti with the Bolognese sauce over the top. Garnish with grated cheese and enjoy.

NOTE: Should the sauce not seem thick enough once cooked, simmer for a bit. Use the BROWN/SAUTÉ setting on LOW. Once desired thickness is achieved, stop cooking.

Sausage and Peppers

Prep time: 15 minutes
Cook time: 2-5 hours (dependent on timing preference – High or Low)
Yield: 8-12 servings, dependent on portion size

Ingredients:
- 1 Tbsp. olive oil
- 1 lb. bulk ground sweet sausage
- ½ lb. lean ground beef
- 2 (15 oz.) cans fire roasted tomatoes
- 1 (8 oz.) can tomato sauce
- 1 small onion, sliced
- 1 red pepper, sliced
- 1 green pepper, sliced
- Sliced provolone or mozzarella
- Fresh rolls

Instructions:
1. Use the BROWN/SAUTÉ setting and brown the sausage and ground beef in the cook pot. Break meat down to bite-size pieces.
2. Add roasted tomatoes, onion, tomato sauce and peppers into the cooker with the sausage mixture.
3. For slow cook, set Slow Cooker LOW with a 5-hour timer. For faster cook, set Slow Cooker HIGH with a 2-hour timer.
4. Toast bread with a slice of cheese on each. Serve sausage and peppers over rolls for open-faced sandwich presentation. Enjoy!

Meatloaf

Prep time: 10 minutes
Cook time: 2-3 hours
Yield: 6-8 serving

Ingredients:

- 2 eggs, beaten
- ¾ cup milk
- ¾ cup dry breadcrumbs
- 1 (1 ounce) envelope dry onion soup mix
- 2 lbs. lean ground beef

Instructions:

1. Line cook pot with parchment paper or foil to help with removal of the meatloaf when finished cooking.
2. Combine eggs, breadcrumbs, milk and dry soup in a large bowl, and mix well.
3. Add ground beef to bowl and blend thoroughly.
4. Form mixed meat into a loaf that will not touch sides of cook pot. Place in cook pot.
5. Cover and cook on Slow Cooker HIGH for 2-3 hours.
6. Once finished, remove meatloaf, slice and serve.
7. If preferred, you can add tomato paste or sauce to the top of the meatloaf about 30 minutes before done.

Party Meatballs

Prep time: 5 minutes
Cook time: 2.5-3 hours
Yield: 4 servings

Ingredients:
- 24 oz. chili sauce
- 1 ½ cup grape jelly
- 2 Tbsp. Worcestershire sauce
- 3 lbs. frozen meatballs

Instructions:
1. Add all liquid ingredients in the cook pot and stir until mixed well.
2. Add meatballs and stir to coat thoroughly.
3. Cook on Slow Cooker LOW for 2 hours.
4. For faster cooking, set to MEAT and cook for 30-45 minutes. Make sure the Steam Release Valve is set to Sealed.
5. Once complete, you can set the cooker to WARM and allow for self-service during party.

Poultry Recipes (Chicken and Turkey)

Sweet and Sour Chicken

Prep time: 15 minutes
Cook time: 1-5.5 hours (based on desired timing – High or Low)
Yield: 6 serving

Ingredients:
- 4 Tbsp. butter, melted
- ¾ cup ketchup
- ½ cup white vinegar
- ¾ cup brown sugar
- 3 Tbsp. Worcestershire sauce
- 2 cloves garlic, minced
- Dash of salt and pepper, to taste
- Dash red pepper flakes or ground cayenne pepper
- 1 ½ cups chicken broth
- 6 boneless chicken breast halves, skin removed
- 1 can (8 or 9 oz.) pineapple chunks, drained
- 1 bell pepper, cut into strips (optional)

Instructions:
1. Place chicken in cook pot.
2. In a large bowl, combine melted butter, ketchup, vinegar, brown sugar, Worcestershire sauce, minced garlic, salt and pepper, hot pepper, and chicken broth. Pour over chicken.
3. Cover and cook on Slow Cooker LOW for 5 hours, until chicken is tender but still moist. For faster cooking, use the POULTRY setting with a 30-minute timer. Make sure the Steam Release Valve is set to Sealed. (If chicken is not tender/moist after 30 minutes, cook on POULTRY setting for 15 more minutes.)
4. If using pineapple and bell pepper, add to cook pot and cook for 20 minutes more using Slow Cooker LOW setting.
5. Serve with/over rice, or with veggies, and enjoy!

Pulled chicken

Prep time: 20 minutes
Cook time: 1-5 hours
Yield: Servings varies by portion size

Ingredients:
- 1 medium onion, finely chopped
- 1 clove garlic, minced
- 1 Tbsp. olive oil (avocado oil, coconut oil or butter may be substituted)
- 1 small can of tomato paste
- ½ cup apricot preserves (pineapple or peach preserves can be substituted)
- 3 Tbsp. cider vinegar
- 2 Tbsp. Worcestershire sauce
- 2 tsp. liquid smoke
- 2 Tbsp. molasses
- Dash of all-spice
- ¼ tsp. freshly ground black pepper
- ¼ tsp. ground cayenne pepper (or to taste)
- 1 lb. boneless chicken breasts
- 1 lb. boneless chicken thighs

Instructions:
1. Using the BROWN/SAUTÉ setting, sauté chopped onions, stirring consistently, until soft and lightly browned. Sauté for 6-10 minutes, making sure not to scorch onions. Add minced garlic and sauté for another 1-2 minutes, again avoiding over-browning by stirring constantly.
2. Add the tomato paste, apricot preserves, vinegar, Worcestershire sauce, liquid smoke, molasses, allspice, black pepper, and cayenne pepper to the onion and garlic.
3. Bring to a simmer and cook for 5 minutes longer, stirring frequently.
4. Remove 1½ cups of the resulting sauce. Pour the remaining sauce into a bowl or storage container, cover and place in fridge for later. Return the 1½ cups of sauce to the cook pot.
5. Add chicken pieces to the cook pot.
6. Cover and cook on Slow Cooker LOW for 4 ½ to 5 hours, or until the chicken is very tender and shreds easily. For faster cooking, use the POULTRY setting with a 1-hour timer. Ensure that the Steam Release Valve is set to Sealed.
7. Once chicken is finished cooking, using two forks, shred the chicken pieces.
8. Serve the pulled chicken on toasted buns with coleslaw and extra barbecue sauce.

Southern Chicken and Biscuits

Prep time: 10 minutes
Cook time: 6.5 hours
Yield: 4 servings

Ingredients:
- 1 ½ to 2 lbs. boneless chicken breast halves, cut into large chunks
- ½ cup chopped onion
- 1 cup chopped celery
- 1 (10 ¾ oz.) can cream of chicken soup, undiluted
- 1 (12 oz.) jar chicken gravy
- ¼ tsp. poultry seasoning
- ½ tsp. dried thyme
- Dash black pepper
- 2 cups frozen mixed vegetables (thawed)
- 6 frozen biscuits (or homemade, see below)

Optional Homemade Southern Biscuits:
- 2 cups all-purpose flour
- 2 ½ tsp. baking powder
- ¼ tsp. baking soda (omit if you use sweet milk)
- 1 tsp. (scant) salt
- 6 Tbsp. butter, chilled
- ¾ cup buttermilk (or sweet milk)

Instructions:
1. In a slow cooker, layer the chunks of uncooked chicken breasts with chopped onion and celery.
2. Combine the soup and gravy with poultry seasoning, thyme, and pepper; pour over the chicken.
3. Cover and cook on LOW for 6 hours.
4. Add the thawed mixed vegetables, turn the slow cooker to HIGH, and continue cooking for 30 minutes, until vegetables are tender.
5. Meanwhile, bake the biscuits as directed on the package or prepare homemade biscuits (see below).
6. To serve, split a biscuit and spoon some of the chicken and vegetables over the bottom half. Put the top half of the biscuit on the chicken and gravy.

Optional Homemade Biscuit Instructions (Serves: 6):

1. In a food processor combine the flour, baking powder, and baking soda (if using buttermilk). Pulse a few times to combine the ingredients. Cut the chilled butter into pieces and add to the food processor. Pulse several times, or until the mixture is the texture of coarse meal. Add the buttermilk or milk and pulse just until the dough begins to form.

2. Turn the dough out onto a floured surface and knead just until the dough comes together. Do not overwork the dough. Pat the dough into a circle or square about 3/4-inch thick and cut out with round or square biscuit cutters.

3. Arrange the biscuits about 2 inches apart on an ungreased or parchment paper-lined baking sheet.

4. Bake in a preheated 425 F oven for about 12 to 15 minutes, or until the tops are lightly browned.

Creamy Chicken and Asparagus

Prep time: 10 minutes
Cook time: 5 hours
Yield: 2 servings

Ingredients:
- 1 ½ lbs. boneless chicken breasts (about 4 to 6 halves)
- ½ cup chicken stock
- 1 (10 ½ oz.) can fat-free cream of onion soup
- Optional: ¼ to ½ tsp. dried leaf tarragon
- 1 tsp. lemon pepper seasoning (or another kind of herb seasoning)
- ¼ tsp. salt (or to taste)
- Dash black pepper (or to taste)
- 1 bunch fresh asparagus
- 1 Tbsp. cornstarch
- 1 Tbsp. of cold water
- Optional: Toasted almonds or buttered breadcrumbs (see below)
- Optional: Grated or shredded Parmesan cheese

Instructions:
1. Cut chicken breasts into bite-size chunks and add to the cook pot.
2. Using a large bowl, combine chicken broth, onion soup, tarragon, and lemon pepper seasoning. Mix well and pour over the chicken.
3. Cover and set to Slow Cooker LOW with a 4-hour timer. Alternatively, for a shorter cook time, use the POULTRY setting with a 1-hour timer. When done, the chicken should be tender and thoroughly cooked. Taste sauce and add salt/pepper for desired taste.
4. Cut fresh asparagus into pieces (1-inch), then add it to the chicken.
5. Combine the cornstarch and cold water in a small bowl and stir until the mixture is smooth.
6. Slowly stir the cornstarch mixture into the cook pot.
7. Set to Slow Cooker HIGH and continue cooking for another 10 to 15 minutes. Dish will be done when liquid has thickened, and asparagus is fork tender.
8. Serve hot over noodles or rice. Garnish with Buttery Toasted Breadcrumbs (see below), toasted almonds or Parmesan cheese as desired.

Buttery Toasted Breadcrumbs:
1. Add 2 slices of bread, torn into pieces, to a food processer.
2. Pulse to make coarse crumbs. Toss crumbs with a tablespoon of melted butter (or olive oil) and salt (if desired).
3. You can use the BROWN/SAUTÉ setting to brown the breadcrumbs. Alternatively, a small skillet can be used. Make sure to stir breadcrumbs constantly to avoid scorching or burning.

Turkey Chili

Prep time: 15 minutes
Cook time: 0.5-3 hours (dependent on desired timing – High or Low)
Yield: 6-8 servings

Ingredients:

- 1 lb. lean ground turkey
- 2 chopped green peppers
- 4 cloves minced garlic
- 1 chopped yellow onion
- 1 (28 oz.) can of diced tomatoes
- 1 (14 oz.) can of tomato sauce
- ¼ cup chili powder

Instructions:

1. Set cooker to BROWN/SAUTÉ and add ground turkey. Sauté until no more pink meat is visible.
2. Add the rest of the ingredients to the cooked turkey in the cook pot.
3. Set to Slow Cooker HIGH with a 3-hour timer. For shorter cook time, set to MEAT/STEW High with a 30-minute timer. Ensure the Steam Release Valve is set to Sealed.
4. Once complete, serve with warm bread or crackers and enjoy.

Turkey Breast

Prep time: 10-12 minutes
Cook time: 2 hours
Yield: 8-12 servings

Ingredients:
- 1 (5-6 lbs.) bone-in turkey breast completely thawed
- 5 stalks celery
- 2 medium yellow onions (1 rough-cut in large pieces, 1 cut in half)
- 12-15 baby carrots
- 1 cup chicken broth
- 6 Tbsp. butter (separate 4 Tbsp. and 2 Tbsp.)

Seasonings:
- 1 Tbsp. minced garlic
- 1 tsp. seasoned salt
- 1 tsp. paprika
- ½ tsp. pepper
- 1 tsp. Italian seasoning
- ¼ tsp. dried parsley
- ¼ tsp. dried sage
- Optional: ¼ tsp. dried thyme

Instructions:
1. Ensure that turkey breast is completely thawed. 48 hours in the refrigerator should be sufficient. Do not thaw in cook pot. Pat the turkey down with paper towels.
2. Remove skin from turkey breast. If desired, leave skin intact.
3. Spray the cook pot with non-stick cooking spray or wipe down with olive oil.
4. Place celery stalks, rough-cut onion and baby carrots in cook pot. Pour chicken stock over vegetables.
5. Place the turkey BREAST DOWN over the top of the vegetables. Ensure the turkey is ELEVATED by the vegetables and not contacting the bottom of cook pot.
6. Take the half-cut onion and place inside the turkey breast with 4 Tbsp. butter.
7. Mix all the seasonings together and rub the turkey down. Should you have left the skin on, make sure and rub seasonings UNDER skin.

8. Melt the last 2 Tbsp. of butter. Use a pastry brush and coat the turkey breast.
9. Cover and set cooker with POULTRY setting, Low pressure, with a 2-hour cook time. Ensure that the Steam Release Valve is set to Sealed. When done, check that internal temperature has reached 165 degrees.
10. Remove the turkey from the cook pot and place on platter, breast up.
11. You can remove the large bones from the breast as desired. Carve turkey into slices and serve. Turkey serves well with warm gravy. Enjoy!

Turkey Meatballs

Prep time: 30 minutes
Cook time: 45 minutes – 4 hours (dependent on desired timing – High or Low)
Yield: Servings varies based on portion size

Ingredients:
- 1 large egg
- 2 lbs. extra lean ground turkey
- 2/3 cup Panko bread crumbs
- 3 Tbsp. olive oil
- ¼ cup grated parmesan cheese
- 3 cloves garlic, minced
- 2 tsp. dried oregano
- 2 tsp. dried basil
- 1 tsp. salt
- ½ tsp. fresh ground black pepper
- 1 large onion sweet onion, sliced
- 2 28 oz. cans crushed tomatoes
- Optional: Chopped fresh basil for serving

Instructions:
1. Beat the egg in a large mixing bowl.
2. Add the ground turkey, bread crumbs, garlic, basil, parmesan, 2 Tbsp. olive oil, salt, and pepper. Mix everything to combine, but avoid overmixing.
3. Roll into balls about the size of a golf ball. Place meatballs on a large baking sheet.
4. Use the BROWN/SUATÉ setting; add 1 Tbsp. olive oil and brown the meatballs a few at a time, returning to baking sheet once browned.
5. Once meatballs are browned, add onion slices to the cook pot and top with 1 can of crushed tomatoes.
6. Layer meatballs into the cook pot. Once all browned meatballs have been added to the cook pot, pour second can of crushed tomatoes on top.
7. Cover and set Slow Cooker High with a 4-hour timer. For faster cooking, use the POULTRY setting, high pressure, with a 45-minute timer. Make sure Steam Release Valve is set to Sealed.
8. Meatballs can be served over pasta or can be made into meatball subs. Use chopped basil as garnish to accent flavor.
9. Leftovers can hold in the refrigerator for up to 1 week.

Make-ahead Options: Brown meatballs and store in refrigerator for up to 24 hours, or kept in freezer for up to 2 months. Meatballs in sauce can be kept frozen for up to 60 days. Place in cooker with setting Slow Cooker HIGH for up to 45 minutes to thaw and bring to serving temperature.

Turkey Stroganoff

Prep time: 30-minutes
Cook time: 1-4.25 hours
Yield: 8-10 servings

Ingredients:
- 8 cups sliced mushrooms (about 20 ounces)
- 3 medium carrots, sliced
- 1 small onion, finely chopped
- 1 (3-4 lb.) split turkey breast, trimmed w/skin removed
- 1 cup reduced-fat sour cream
- 1/3 cup all-purpose flour
- ¼ cup dry sherry (can substitute cooking sherry)
- 1 cup frozen peas, thawed
- 1 tsp. salt (if using cooking sherry, omit salt)
- ½ tsp. freshly ground pepper
- 8 oz. whole-wheat egg noodles (6 cups dry), cooked
- ¼ cup finely chopped flat-leaf parsley

Instructions:
1. Combine mushrooms, carrots and onion in the cook pot.
2. Place turkey over vegetables, breast side down.
3. Close lid and set to Slow Cooker HIGH with a 4-hour timer. For faster cooking, use the POULTRY setting, high pressure, with a 1-hour timer. Ensure the Steam Release Valve is set to Sealed.
4. When cooking has completed, place turkey on a cutting board.
5. In a bowl, whisk together the sour cream, flour and sherry. Stir into the cook pot, and add the peas, salt and pepper.
6. Cover and cook on Slow Cooker HIGH until thickened; roughly 15 minutes.
7. Carve the turkey from the bone and dice into bite-size pieces. When the sauce has thickened, gently stir in the turkey.

Serve over noodles, garnished with parsley.

Make Ahead Tip: Prep turkey and vegetables; cover and refrigerate separately for up to 1 day.

Sherry Tip: Dry sherry is preferred over cooking sherry. Dry sherry adds strong flavor to sauces and dishes like stroganoff; however, does not include the salt content that cooking sherry contains. Dry sherry can be found in the fortified wines section of your grocery store or liquor store.

Sticky Wings

Prep time: 30 minutes
Cook time: 30 minutes – 3.5 hours (dependent on preferred timing – High or Low)
Yield: Serving varies by portion size

Ingredients:
- ¾ cup packed dark brown sugar
- ¼ cup soy sauce
- 3-inch piece fresh ginger, peeled and roughly chopped
- 4 garlic cloves, peeled
- ½ tsp. cayenne pepper
- 4 lbs. chicken wings, halved at joint (discard wing tips)
- ¼ cup water
- ¼ cup tomato paste

Instructions:
1. Add ¼ cup of the brown sugar, 1 Tbsp. of the soy sauce, ginger, garlic and 1/4 tsp. cayenne pepper to a food processor. Pulse to grind fine, until a paste-like mixture results. Transfer the mixture to the cook pot.
2. Add the wings and stir until well-coated with sauce.
3. Use the POULTRY setting, high pressure, with a 30-minute cook time. Make sure the Steam Release Valve is set to Sealed. If you prefer slow cooking, use the Slow Cooker LOW setting with a 3-hour timer.
4. Once cooked, place the wings in a large bowl. Drain wings well as they are removed to minimize liquid transfer. Once all wings are removed, discard liquid.
5. Cool wings for approximately 20 minutes.
6. Preheat broiler oven, placing a rack near top, 10-12 inches from element. Line a large baking sheet with foil, add a wire baking rack, and spray with non-stick cook spray.
7. In another bowl, whisk together the remaining sugar, water, tomato paste, remaining soy sauce and cayenne pepper. Place half of this sauce in large bowl with wings. Toss wings until coated well; gently to prevent tearing chicken.
8. Lay wings out on rack; can be spaced close together to allow all wings to fit on pan. Broil for up to 15 minutes, checking every 3-4 minutes (more often once close to done), and browning well (light char). Take wings from broiler, turn all wings over on rack. Brush on remaining sauce and place back in broiler. Cook for another 3-4 minutes, checking regularly that sauce is caramelized.
9. Remove and serve hot with celery/blue cheese, French fries or your preferred side. Enjoy!

Chicken and Biscuits

Prep time: 20 minutes
Cook time: 55 minutes – 3 hours (dependent on timing preference – High or Low)
Yield: 8-10 servings

Ingredients:

- ¾ lb. carrots (about 4), cut into 1-inch lengths
- 2 stalks celery, thinly sliced
- 1 small onion, chopped
- ¼ cup all-purpose flour
- 1 ½ lb. boneless, skinless chicken breast halves (about 8)
- ½ tsp. poultry seasoning
- 1 tsp. kosher salt
- ¼ tsp. black pepper
- ½ cup dry white wine
- ½ cup low-sodium chicken broth
- 6 biscuits, baked and split
- 1 cup frozen peas
- ½ cup heavy cream

Instructions:

1. Toss carrots, onion, celery and flour together in cook pot.
2. Place chicken breasts over floured vegetables and season with poultry seasoning, kosher salt and black pepper. Then pour in white wine and chicken broth.
3. Cover and use POULTRY setting with a 45-minute timer. Ensure the Steam Release Valve is set to Sealed. For slow cooking, set to Slow Cooker HIGH for 2.5 hours, or until chicken and vegetables are tender.
4. Approximately 30 minutes before chicken is finished, cook biscuits. You can choose to make your own or canned biscuits will suffice.
5. When cooking is complete, use two forks and tear chicken into bite size pieces.
6. Return chicken to cook pot. Stir in peas, cream and ½ tsp. salt. Cover and cook (Slow Cooker HIGH) until heated through, 5 to 10 minutes more.
7. To serve, place bottom half of a biscuit in a bowl, cover with chicken/vegetables and top with second half of biscuit. Enjoy!

Seafood Dishes

Jambalaya

Prep time: 15 minutes
Cook time: 1.25-3.5 hours
Yield: 6-8 servings

Ingredients:
- 1 large onion, chopped (about 1 cup)
- 1 medium green bell pepper, chopped (about 1 cup)
- 2 medium celery stalks, chopped (about 1 cup)
- 3 garlic cloves, finely chopped
- 1 (28 oz.) can diced tomatoes, undrained
- 2 cups smoked sausage, chopped fully cooked
- 1 Tbsp. parsley flakes
- ½ tsp. dried thyme leaves
- ½ tsp. salt
- ¼ tsp. pepper
- ¼ tsp. red pepper sauce
- ¾ lb. medium shrimp, (thawed, uncooked, peeled, and deveined)

Instructions:
1. Mix all ingredients EXCEPT shrimp in cook pot.
2. Cover and set to Slow Cooker HIGH with a 3-hour timer. For faster cooking, use the MEAT/STEW setting, low pressure, with a 45-minute timer. Make sure Steam Release Valve is set to Sealed.
3. Once cooking is complete, stir in shrimp. Cover and cook on Slow Cooker HIGH setting with a 30-minute timer, or until shrimp is firm and pink.
4. Serve with rice and enjoy.

Salmon Chowder

Prep time: 15-20 minutes
Cook time: 45 minutes - 2.5 hours (dependent on timing preference – High or Low)
Yield: 6-8 servings

Ingredients:

- 8 oz. red potatoes, diced into 1/2-inch chunks
- 8 oz. frozen corn
- 15 oz. can low-fat creamed corn
- 1 small onion, diced
- 1 medium red bell pepper, seeded and diced
- 1 jalapeno pepper, seeded and diced
- 2 cups vegetable or seafood stock
- 1 tsp. seafood seasoning, such as Old Bay
- 2 (5 oz.) cans salmon, drained (or 1 cup leftover cooked salmon, flaked)
- 1 cup cream or half and half
- 3-5 dashes hot sauce (optional)
- 4-6 slices bacon, cooked, for garnish

Instructions:

1. Place frozen corn, creamed corn, potatoes, jalapeno and red peppers, onions, seafood seasoning and vegetable stock into the cook pot.
2. Cover and set to Slow Cooker HIGH with a 2-hour timer. For faster cooking, use the SOUP setting with a 30-minute timer. Ensure the Steam Release Valve is set to Sealed.
3. When finished cooking, place half the vegetable/sauce mix into a blender. Cover with a hand towel to prevent steam burns with lid. Puree soup mixture until thickened. Carefully pour back into cook pot.
4. Stir in salmon, cream/half and half and optional hot sauce.
5. Set to Slow Cooker HIGH and cook for 15-30 minutes. Check taste and add more seasoning if desired. Flavors can be muted, so adjust accordingly.
6. Serve in bowls with chopped bacon bits as garnish. Enjoy!

Poached Salmon

Prep time: 45 minutes
Cook time: 1 hour
Yield: 3-6 servings (varies with portion size and fillet size)

Ingredients:
For Poaching Liquid:
- 6 cups water
- 1 medium onion, chopped
- 2 stalks celery, chopped (can substitute ½ tsp. celery seed)
- 4 sprigs parsley
- ½ cup white wine or freshly squeezed lemon juice
- 8 wholes black peppercorns
- 1 bay leaf

For Salmon:
- 1 fillet salmon
- Lemon slices (for garnish)
- Springs of fresh parsley or dill (for garnish)

Instructions:
Make Ahead Tip: Poaching liquid can be made in advance and held. Cover and refrigerate for up to 48 hours.

For Poaching Liquid:
1. Using a medium sauce pan, combine onion, parsley, white wine, water, celery, peppercorns, and bay leaf over medium heat.
2. Bring to a boil and simmer for 30 minutes. Strain liquid, discarding solids. Return liquid to sauce pan and bring back to boil while preparing salmon.

For Salmon:
1. Line bottom and up sides of cook pot with folded aluminum foil. Lay salmon fillet on foil in cook pot.
2. When poaching liquid has returned to a boil, pour over salmon. Salmon should be covered completely. If liquid does not fully cover salmon, add some water to achieve level.
3. Close cooker and set to Slow Cooker HIGH with a 1-hour timer. Do not attempt a fast-cook method, as this can easily overcook the salmon.
4. When cooking is finished, salmon will be firm to the touch and skin peels off easily. Remove cook pot and let stand/cool for 20 minutes. If serving hot, remove salmon from liquid and place on platter to serve.
5. Salmon can be served cold if preferred. If so, place covered cook pot (salmon and liquid) in refrigerator until fully chilled.
6. Garnish with lemon slices and parsley or dill and serve. Enjoy!

Salmon Loaf

Prep time: 10 minutes
Cook time: 2.5-5 hours (depends on preferred cook time – High or Low)
Yield: 6 servings

Ingredients:
- 2 eggs, lightly beaten
- 2 cups seasoned stuffing croutons
- 1 cup chicken stock
- 1 cup grated Parmesan cheese
- ¼ tsp. ground mustard
- 1 lb. salmon, deboned, chopped/minced well to a "ground" consistency

Instructions:
1. Combine eggs, croutons, stock, Parmesan and mustard in a medium bowl.
2. Mix salmon into bowl. Mixture should be "dry" and moldable.
3. Spray the cook pot with non-stick cooking spray or coat with olive oil. Place the salmon mixture in the cook pot.
4. Gently shape mixture into a loaf, making sure it does not touch sides of cook pot if possible.
5. Set cooker to Slow Cooker LOW with a 4-5-hour timer, or Slow Cooker HIGH with a 2.5-hour timer.
6. Once finished, let stand for 15 minutes, then remove gently transfer from cook pot to platter.
7. Garnish of lemon slices or dill add a tasty finish.
8. Slice, serve and enjoy!

Paella

Prep time: 15-20 minutes
Cook time: 2-5 hours (depending on preference – High or Low)
Yield: 6-8 servings

Ingredients:

- 1 ½ cups of the long grain brown rice
- ½ lb. lean ground sausage (sliced kielbasa can be substituted)
- 1 onion
- 1 green pepper
- 4 garlic cloves, crushed
- 1 ½ lbs. of chicken (boneless skinless chicken breast)
- 1 lb. of medium shrimp
- 1 can of Rotel tomatoes
- ½ tsp. of Turmeric
- ¼ tsp. of Paprika
- 1 ½ cup of chicken broth
- 2 tsp. of salt
- Optional: 1 bag of frozen peas

Instructions:

1. Use the BROWN/SAUTÉ setting and brown the sausage and drain grease.
2. Add the rest of ingredients, EXCEPT for shrimp, into the cook pot.
3. Set cooker to Slow Cooker LOW and cook for 4-5 hours, or use Slow Cooker HIGH with a 2-hour timer. Begin to check rice about 30 minutes before done to check doneness. Avoid overcooking the rice, as it will get mushy.
4. Add the shrimp in for the last 20 minutes of cook time. Shrimp should be firm and pink when cooked properly.
5. If you choose to include peas, add in after cook cycle is done and cooker goes in to KEEP WARM mode. Peas will be ready in 5-10 minutes after adding.
6. Serve with warm bread, or alone. Enjoy!

Seafood Dip

Prep time: 15 minutes
Cook time: 1 hour
Yield: Serving varies by portion size

Ingredients:
- 8 oz. cream cheese, softened
- ½ cup low-fat mayonnaise
- 3 green onions, chopped
- 2 cloves garlic, minced
- 2 Tbsp. lemon juice
- ¼ cup tomato paste
- 8 oz. shrimp, deveined and chopped fine
- Vegetable dippers or crackers

Instructions:
1. In a medium bowl, mix mayonnaise, green onions, garlic, cream cheese, tomato paste and lemon juice together thoroughly.
2. Add chopped shrimp to bowl, mashing with a fork as you mix. Salt and pepper to taste.
3. Pour mixture into the cook pot.
4. Set the cooker to Slow Cooker HIGH with a 1-hour timer.
5. Serve w/vegetable dippers or crackers, or both.

Shrimp Scampi

Prep time: 20 minutes
Cook time: 15 minutes
Yield: 4-6 servings

Ingredients:
- 1 lb. large raw shrimp (31/35 count), peeled, deveined if desired
- 1 (12 oz.) package angel hair pasta
- ½ cup butter
- ¼ cup finely chopped onion
- 3 garlic cloves, finely chopped
- 1 tsp. salt-free Italian-herb seasoning
- 1 tsp. Worcestershire sauce
- 1 Tbsp. fresh lemon juice
- ¼ cup freshly grated Romano or Parmesan cheese
- 1 Tbsp. chopped fresh parsley

Instructions:
1. Prepare angel hair pasta according to package directions and set aside.
2. Using the BROWN/SAUTÉ setting, melt butter in cook pot, then sauté the onion and garlic for 3-5 minutes or until tender. Mix in the Italian-herb seasoning and Worcestershire sauce.
3. Lower temperature on cooker and add shrimp. Sauté the shrimp, stirring frequently to prevent over cooking for about 3-5 minutes. Shrimp will turn pink when done.
4. Stir the lemon juice into the shrimp.
5. Toss the shrimp mixture with angel hair pasta. Finish with grated cheese and parsley.
6. Serve immediately. Enjoy!

Sides-Dips-Appetizers

Buffalo Chicken Dip

Prep time: 20 minutes
Cook time: 1.5 hours
Yield: Serving varies with portion size

Ingredients:
- 2 ½ cups cooked, shredded chicken (rotisserie chicken works well)
- ½ cup hot sauce
- 8 oz. low fat cream cheese
- ½ cup ranch dressing, homemade or store bought
- ½ cup cheddar cheese shredded
- ½ cup feta or blue cheese crumbles

Instructions:
1. Stir together all ingredients until well-combined in the cook pot.
2. Set cooker to Slow Cooker LOW for 1½ hours or until cheese is melted and dip starts to bubble on edges. Stir regularly to ensure even cooking.
3. Serve with your favorite chips, crackers, and/or veggies.

Bean Dip

Prep time: 10 minutes
Cook time: 1 hour
Yield: Serving varies with portion size

Ingredients:
- 1 (15 oz.) can refried beans
- 1 cup picante sauce (your choice)
- 1 cup shredded Monterey jack cheese
- 1 cup shredded cheddar cheese
- ¾ cup sour cream
- 1 (3 oz.) package cream cheese, softened
- 1 tablespoon chili powder
- ¼ tsp. ground cumin
- Tortilla chips
- Salsa

Instructions:
1. In a bowl, mix all the ingredients minus the Tortilla chips and salsa.
2. Transfer to the cook pot.
3. Cover and set cooker to Slow Cooker HIGH for 1-hour or until heated through. Stir occasionally to prevent drying or burning.
4. Serve with chips and salsa.

Macaroni and Cheese

Prep time: 20 minutes
Cook time: 1.5 hours
Yield: 4-6 servings

Ingredients:
- 1 (8 oz.) box macaroni
- 1 stick butter
- 2 ½ cups cheddar; sharp, grated
- 2 egg
- 1 large can evaporated milk
- 1 ½ cup milk
- Salt
- Pepper

Instructions:
1. Cook and drain macaroni, then place in cook pot.
2. Add butter and cheddar cheese, then stir.
3. In medium bowl, beat eggs, milk, evaporated milk, salt and pepper together until well mixed. Stir into cook pot.
4. Top with ½ cup cheese.
5. Cover cook pot. Set cooker to Slow Cooker HIGH with a 1.5 hour timer.
6. Serve as side with dinner. Enjoy.

White Queso Dip

Prep time: 10 minutes
Cook time: 45 minutes - 2 hours (depending on preference – High or Low)
Yield: Serving varies by portion size

Ingredients:
- 2 lbs. VELVEETA Queso Blanco (low or fat-free, preferred)
- 1 cup milk
- 2 Tbsp. butter
- 1 (4 oz.) can diced green chilies, undrained
- 2 Tbsp. diced pickled jalapeños
- ½ tsp. Taco seasoning
- ¼ tsp. garlic powder
- Tortilla chips

Instructions:
1. Cut cheese into cubes and place into the cook pot.
2. Add in milk and butter.
3. Pour in can of undrained, diced green chilies.
4. Add finely chopped jalapeno peppers to the cook pot. Add in taco seasoning and garlic powder.
5. Stir all to blend together, coating cheese cubes.
6. Set cooker to Slow Cooker LOW with a 2-hour timer, or use Slow Cooker HIGH with a 45-minute timer.

IMPORTANT NOTE: It is essential to monitor cheese dip as it cooks. Stir occasionally, using caution when opening cooker, to prevent burning on sides. Cheese should be warm and bubbly. Stop cooker early if dip appears to be browning along sides.

Hummus

Prep time: 30-45 minutes prep time
Cook time: 15 minutes cook time
Yield: Serving varies by portion size

Ingredients:

- 4 cups homemade chickpeas made from 1 cup dry chickpeas (frozen pressure cooker chickpeas can be substituted)
- 4 cups water (if cooking the chickpeas)
- 2 medium cloves garlic, peeled
- ½ tsp. kosher salt
- ½ cup chickpea cooking liquid (reserved from cooking the chickpeas, or water if you 're using canned)
- Juice of 1 lemon
- ¼ cup tahini (or substitute natural peanut butter)
- ½ cup extra virgin olive oil
- Salt and pepper, to taste
- Paprika (for color; smoked Spanish paprika, pimenton de la vera, is my favorite)

Instructions:

For Homemade Chickpea:

1. Place 1 cup of dry chickpeas and 4 cups of water in the cook pot. Close the lid.
2. Use the BEANS/CHILI setting on HIGH with a 15-minute timer. Make sure the Steam Release Valve is set to the Sealed position. Once finished and pressure has released, check the beans for tenderness. (if not quite tender, use the Slow Cooker HIGH setting and cook for 15 minutes more) Once chickpeas are done, drain liquid making sure to save ½ cup to the side.

NOTE: Frozen, pressure cooker chickpeas (thaw before using in cooker). Not recommended: You can substitute 2 cans of

For Hummus Instructions:

1. Using a food processor, chop garlic thoroughly for about 30 seconds. Next, add the chickpeas and kosher salt. Blend until chickpeas are ground. This should require about 5-6, one second pulses.
2. Add the liquid from the cooked chickpeas (use ½ cup water if using pre-made chickpeas), tahini, and lemon juice. Mix in processor for 15 seconds. Scrape the chickpea mixture from the sides and center in processor, then mix again for 15

seconds, ensuring everything is combined well and very thick. Scrap sides down again before next step.

3. Start the processor again. Slowly drizzle olive oil through the tube; maintain slow, steady stream. Once the oil has been added, continue running for 30 seconds or hummus achieves a smooth, fluffy consistency.

4. Check the flavor and season with salt and pepper to taste. Place the hummus in a serving dish and garnish with a dash of paprika and drizzle of olive oil. Serve with pita wedges, pita chips or dipping vegetables like carrots and celery.

Party Snacks

Prep time: 10 minutes
Cook time: 2 hours
Yield: Serving varies by portion size

Ingredients:

- 3 cups bite-size crispy rice cereal
- 2 cups o-shaped toasted oat cereal
- 2 cups bite size shredded whole wheat cereal
- 1 cup pecans
- 1 cup thin pretzel stick
- ½ cup butter
- 4 Tbsp. Worcestershire sauce
- ½ tsp. seasoning salt
- ½ tsp. garlic salt
- ½ tsp. onion salt
- 1 dash hot pepper sauce

Instructions:

1. Combine nuts, pretzels and cereals in cook pot.
2. In small bowl, mix the melted butter and remaining ingredients. Pour over mixture in cook pot, toss lightly to coat.
3. Cover cook pot and set to Slow Cooker LOW with a 2-hour timer. Stir the mix every 15 minutes to keep blended. Watch that mix does not get too hot and burns.
4. Once finished, let cool completely. Store in a sealed container to prevent from getting stale.
5. Enjoy!

Vegetarian Recipes

Vegetarian Lasagna

Prep time: 30-35 minutes
Cook time: 5 hours
Yield: 6-8 servings

Ingredients:
- 2 Tbsp. olive oil
- 2 onions, diced
- 3 garlic cloves, crushed
- 2 (6 oz.) cans tomato paste
- 2 cans tomato sauce
- 1 ½ tsp. salt
- 1 ½ tsp. pepper
- 1 ½ cups mushrooms, sliced
- 1 tsp. dried oregano
- 1 container ricotta cheese
- 4 cups fresh spinach, rinsed
- ½ cup Parmesan cheese (or ½ cup Asiago cheese, grated)
- 2 boxes no-boil lasagna noodles (oven ready, uncooked)
- 16 oz. mozzarella cheese, shredded

Instructions:
1. Using the BROWN/SAUTÉ setting, add the olive oil, onions and garlic to the cook pot. Sauté until onions and garlic are tender; 3-4 minutes. Add the mushrooms, salt, pepper and oregano. Continue cooking for another 3 minutes with constant stirring to avoid burning.
2. Next, thoroughly stir in tomato paste, then the tomato sauce. Stirring occasionally, cook the sauce for about 6-8 minutes till completely heated. Once done, pour sauce into large bowl.
3. Ladle some sauce back into the cook pot; just enough to cover the bottom. Lay in two layers of lasagna noodles. If necessary, break to accommodate size.
4. For the next layer, add half of the ricotta cheese, ¾ tsp. salt and ¾ tsp. pepper. Then add two layers of noodles.
5. Using half the sauce, cover the noodles, then half of the mozzarella cheese sprinkled over the sauce. Add two layers of noodles.

6. Layer the rest of the ricotta cheese. Shake spinach leaves to remove any remaining water. Layer spinach over chees and add remaining salt and pepper. Two more layers of noodles.
7. Finish with the rest of the sauce, mozzarella and parmesan (or asiago) cheeses.
8. Close the lid. Use the Slow Cook LOW setting with a 4-5-hour timer. When lasagna is done, carefully remove cook pot and allow lasagna to set for at least 10 minutes before serving.

Vegan Applesauce

Prep time: 20 minutes
Cook time: 5 hours
Yield: Varies by batch/portion size

Ingredients:

- 3 lbs. apples, peeled, cored and cut in eighths (try organic gala)
- ¼ cup lemon juice
- 2 tsp. vanilla
- 1 tsp. cinnamon
- 1 Tbsp. brown sugar or sucanat

Instructions:

1. Add all ingredients to the cook pot.
2. Set to Slow Cooker on LOW with a 5-hour timer. Check apples for tenderness (fork mashable). If they still need time, cook for another 15 minutes at a time until consistency achieved.
3. Once cooking is complete, using a potato masher, mash and blend all ingredients well.

Save for Later: Freeze your applesauce for later use in baking, other recipes or meals. Use silicone muffin cups and add about ¼ cup of applesauce to each. Place in freezer to freeze; at least for 4 hours. Once frozen, move applesauce from muffin tins to plastic freezer bags. Best to use them within 30-60 days.

If needed as an egg or oil substitute, pop in the microwave for 1 or 2 minutes and applesauce is ready to go.

Vegan Spaghetti Sauce

Prep time: 10 minutes
Cook time: 2-6 hours
Yield: Varies by portion size

Ingredients:
- 1 cup diced onion
- 2 (14 oz.) cans diced tomatoes, undrained
- 6 oz. can tomato paste
- 8 oz. can tomato sauce
- 2 tsp. minced garlic
- 1 ½ Tbsp. Italian seasoning
- 1 tsp. kosher salt
- 1 Tbsp. brown sugar
- 1 bay leaf

Instructions:
1. Add all ingredients to the cook pot. Mix well with a whisk or kitchen spoon.
2. Add the bay leaf on top of the sauce.
3. Use the Slow Cook LOW setting with a 6-hour timer. For faster cooking use Slow Cook HIGH with a 2-3-hour timer. Make sure the Steam Release Valve is set at Release.
4. Once cooking has ended, serve over spaghetti or your preferred pasta. Enjoy!

Spaghetti Squash Marinara

Prep time: 15-20 minutes
Cook time: 15 minutes - 8 hours (depending on desired timing – High or Low)
Yield: 4-5 servings

Ingredients:
- 1 large (approx. 3 lbs.) spaghetti squash
- 1 small onion, diced
- 3 cloves of garlic, minced
- 1 tsp. salt
- 1 tsp. black pepper
- 1 (28 oz.) can of tomato sauce
- 1 cup vegetable stock
- 1 bay leaf
- 1 Tbsp. olive oil
- ¼ cup grated pecorino Romano cheese

Instructions:
1. Using the BROWN/SAUTÉ setting on HIGH. Once hot, add olive oil and onions and sauté for about 2-4 minutes till onions are becoming tender. Next add in garlic, salt and pepper.
2. Stir in vegetable stock, tomato sauce and the bay leaf. Stir until well combined.
3. Next, poke holes in the squash with a large kitchen knife and set the whole squash in the cook pot over the sauce. If you prefer, use the steam rack for stability. Close the lid.
4. Use the Slow Cooker HIGH setting with a 6-8-hour timer. Check that the Steam Release Valve is in the Release position. At 6 hours, begin checking if the squash is tender by trying to pierce it with a fork.

Alternative Fast Cook Method:
1. Use the BEANS/CHILI setting on HIGH with a 15-minute timer. Ensure the Steam Release Valve is in the Sealed position before starting cook cycle.
2. Once cooking is done, and pressure has been released, check that squash can be pierced with a fork. Remove squash from the cook pot, and cut in half. Scrap out the seeds and throw away. Using a fork, remove the flesh from the squash. This should come out in long strands that look like spaghetti.
3. Serve meat from squash like spaghetti with the marinara sauce over the top. Garnish with grated cheese and enjoy.

NOTE: Should the sauce not seem thick enough once cooked, simmer for a bit. Use the BROWN/SAUTÉ setting on LOW. Once desired thickness is achieved, stop cooking.

Minestrone Soup

Prep time: 1 hour (includes cooking corn)
Cook time: 30 minutes - 3 hours (depending on timing desired – High or Low)
Yield: 6-8 servings

Ingredients:
- 4 cups vegetable stock
- 4 cups black beans, cooked
- 5 Roma tomatoes, diced (about 2 cups)
- 2 ears corn, roasted and kernels cut off cob (about 1 cup)
- 8 oz. mushrooms, sliced
- Salt and pepper to taste
- 2 Tbsp. olive oil

Instructions:
For Roasted Corn:
1. Peel corn husks back without removing, and clean silk from corn. Recover with husks.
2. Soak the corn in a bowl of water for 20 minutes. Drain the corn. Cook on grill top or over gas burner for 20-35 minutes. Cover while cooking, and rotate regularly. The husks will be blackened, and corn will be tender to the touch. Allow corn to cool thoroughly, then cut the kernels off.

For Soup:
1. When corn is finished, set cooker to BROWN/SAUTÉ, HIGH heat. Add olive oil and mushrooms to cook pot and sauté for 2-3 minutes.
2. Sauté mushrooms in a bit of olive oil until tender.
3. Stir all remaining ingredients, including corn, to the cook pot. Mix well to combine.
4. Use the SOUP setting, HIGH pressure, with a 30-minute cook time. Make sure Steam Release Valve is in the Sealed position.
5. You can choose a slower cook time. Select Slow Cook HIGH with a 3-hour timer. For this, make sure the Steam Release Valve is in the Release position.
6. Once soup is done, serve and enjoy!

Vegan Purple Mashed Potatoes

Prep time: 15 minutes
Cook time: 2 hours
Yield: 8-10 servings

Ingredients:

- 5 lbs. purple potatoes diced with peel (use new red if preferred)
- 1 cup water
- 1 cup coconut oil
- 1 Tbsp. salt
- ¾ tsp. pepper
- 1 1/3 cups coconut milk, warmed

Instructions:

1. Place the water, coconut oil, and potatoes in the cook pot. Add salt and pepper.
2. Cover and set to Slow Cook HIGH for 2 hours. Make sure the Steam Release Valve is in the Release position.
3. Once cooking is completed, add coconut milk and mash to desired consistency.
4. Serve and enjoy.

Vegan Salsa Chickpeas

Prep time: 5 minutes
Cook time: 45 minutes - 8 hours (depending on desired timing – High or Low)
Yield: Varies by portion size

Ingredients:
- 2 cups dry chickpeas, rinsed
- 1 cup Homemade Salsa
- 16 oz. fresh corn cut from cob, or 15.25 oz. can corn, undrained
- 2 cups vegetable stock
- Enough water to cover chickpeas with about 2 inches of liquid over them

Instructions:
1. Add all ingredients to the cook pot.
2. Use the BEAN/CHILI setting on HIGH with a 45-minute cook time. Make sure the Steam Release Valve is set to Sealed.
3. Once cooking is finished and pressure has released, check chickpeas for tenderness. If they are not tender enough, cook again with a 15-minute timer on the BEAN/CHILI setting.
4. For a longer cook time, use the Slow Cooker LOW setting with an 6-8-hour timer. Make sure Steam Release Valve is in the Release position.
5. Works well as a side dish, as burritos, tacos and wraps.

Brown Sugar Chicken (Seitan)

Prep time: 10 minutes
Cook time: 5 hours
Yield: 4 servings

Ingredients:
- 2 medium green peppers (or 2 medium gypsy peppers), diced
- 1 medium onion, diced
- 16 oz. seitan or other chicken alternative, cubed
- 1 cup brown sugar
- 2/3 cup vinegar
- 4 cloves minced garlic
- 2 Tbsp. soy sauce
- 1 tsp. black pepper
- ¼ to ½ cup ginger ale
- Brown or white rice

Instructions:
1. Add olive oil to bottom of cook pot. Next add onion, green peppers, and seitan.
2. Cover with the rest of the ingredients. If you are using a slow cooker seitan, only use ¼ cup of ginger ale, as there is more liquid present in the seitan. Otherwise, use ½ cup. Pour ginger ale slowly if you want to avoid some bubbling.
3. Cover and use the Slow Cooker LOW setting with a 5-hour timer. Make sure the Steam Release Valve is in the Release position.
4. Once cooking is complete, serve over white or brown rice as preferred.

Cuban Black Bean Soup

Prep time: 10 minutes
Cook time: 45 minutes - 6 hours
Yield: 8-10 servings

Ingredients:

- 16 oz. dry black beans, soaked for 24 hours
- 6 cups vegetable stock
- 1 can organic tomato paste
- 1 can green chilies
- 1 onion, finely chopped
- 3 cloves garlic, minced
- 2 Tbsp. cumin
- 1 Tbsp. red wine vinegar

Instructions:

1. Add all ingredients to the cook pot.
2. Use the Slow Cooker LOW setting with a 6-hour timer. Make sure Steam Release Valve is in Release position.
3. For faster cooking, use the SOUP setting with a 45-minute timer. For this, make sure the Steam Release Valve is in the Sealed position.
4. Once cooked, allow to cool. When cool, use a stick blender or high-speed blender and blend soup to desired consistency.
5. Set the cooker to Slow Cook HIGH for 15 minutes to reheat. Then serve and enjoy!

Eggplant Parmesan

Prep time: 1 hour
Cook time: 2-4.5 hours (depending on timing preference – High or Low)
Yield: 6 servings

Ingredients:

- 3 medium to large eggplant, peeled
- 2 large eggs
- 1/3 cup water
- 3 Tbsp. flour
- 3 Tbsp. extra virgin olive oil
- 1/3 cup seasoned bread crumbs
- ½ cup fresh grated Parmesan cheese
- 32 oz. marinara sauce
- 16 oz. mozzarella cheese, sliced or shredded

Instructions:

1. Cut eggplant in 1/2-inch slices. Line a baking pan with paper towels. Sprinkle salt on both sides of each slice, lay out on lined pan and let dry for 30 minutes.
2. Turn on the cooker using the BROWN/SAUTÉ setting on HIGH and preheat.
3. In a medium bowl, beat the eggs, flour and water together. Once blended well, dip eggplant slices into batter, allowing excess to drip off.
4. Add olive oil to the cook pot, then sauté the eggplant slices until they reach a light, golden brown color on both sides. Once done, turn cooker off and remove cook pot to cool.
5. Mix parmesan cheese and bread crumbs together in a small bowl.
6. Layer eggplant into the bottom of the cook pot; about ¼ of the eggplant. Sprinkle a layer of crumb-cheese mixture, ¼ of the marinara and ¼ of the mozzarella. Repeat layering in this order building to 4 layers in cook pot.
7. Close the lid. Use the Slow Cooker LOW setting with a timer of 4.5 hours. For shorter cooking, set to Slow Cooker HIGH with a 2-hour timer. The Steam Release Valve should be in the Release position. Once finished, check with fork to make sure eggplant is tender.
8. Serve garnished with parmesan cheese and enjoy!

Delicious Desert Recipes

Time for a little indulgence. Everyone can enjoy a little sweet retreat sometimes. Here are some great recipes to tempt your family's taste buds. If you want to adjust to minimize the sugar, most of these recipes allow for sugar substitutes and reduced fat dairy ingredients. Just remember, moderation, moderation, moderation.

Pazookie

Prep time: 15 minutes
Cook time: 1.5 hours
Yield: Varies by portion size

Ingredients:
- 1 pack of chocolate sandwich cookies
- 1 package chocolate chip cookie dough
- 3 Tbsp. butter

Instructions:
1. In a food processor blend 1 and 1/2 rows of sandwich cookies.
2. Next, add in butter and blend into cookie mixture. The resulting cooking crumble should hold shape when picked up and squeezed in your hand.
3. Spread the mixture across the bottom of the cook pot, pressing to form a crust.
4. Cut and place pieces of the cookie dough over the cookie crumble crust, making sure to cover the surface.
5. Set cooker to Slow Cooker HIGH with a timer of 1.5 hours.
6. Once finished, let Pazookie rest and set for 10-15 minutes. It will start out gooey and harden a bit once it sets. **Best served with ice cream and fudge topping.**

Chocolate Spoon Cake

Prep time: 5 minutes
Cook time: 3-4 hours
Yield: 6-8 servings

Ingredients:
- 1 box chocolate cake mix
- 1 (4 oz.) small box instant chocolate pudding mix
- 2 cups sour cream
- ¾ cup vegetable or canola oil
- 4 eggs
- 1 cup water
- 1 cup semi-sweet chocolate chips

Instructions:
1. Spray cook pot with nonstick cooking spray.
2. In a large bowl, combine first six ingredients until combined.
3. Add chocolate chips and mix well.
4. Pour into prepared cook pot.
5. Cover and set to Slow Cooker LOW for 3-4 hours. Check cake at 2.5 hours for doneness, and every 30 minutes after. Cake should spring back when touched if it is ready.
6. Serve warm with whipped cream, ice cream, chocolate syrup or your choice of topping, if desired. Cake will be very rich.

Gingerbread Pudding

Prep time: 15 minutes
Cook time: 2 hours
Yield: 6-8+ servings

Ingredients:
- 14 ½ oz. package gingerbread mix
- ½ cup whole milk
- ½ cup golden raisins
- 2 ¼ cup water
- ¾ cup brown sugar, firmly packed
- ¾ cup butter
- Garnish: vanilla or eggnog ice cream

Instructions:
1. Spray inside of cook pot with non-stick cooking spray.
2. Combine gingerbread mix and milk in medium bowl until just moistened. Add raisins to the mix, which should be thick. Pour and spread batter in bottom of cook pot.
3. Use a medium saucepan and combine water, butter and brown sugar, then bring to a boil. Reduce heat to gentle boil and cook uncovered for 2 minutes. Pour mixture over batter in cook pot.
4. Close lid and set to Slow Cook HIGH with a 2-hour timer. Make sure the Steam Release Valve is set to Release.
5. When done, center will be moist but will firm up when allowed to set.
6. Remove cook pot, leave uncovered and let it cool and set for about 45 minutes.
7. Serve warm pudding with vanilla ice cream, or holiday eggnog ice cream.

Strawberry Cream Cake

Prep time: 15 minutes
Cook time: 1.5 - 3 hours
Yield: 8+ servings

Ingredients:
- 15.25 oz. strawberry cake mix, prepared
- 8 oz. cream cheese
- 1 egg
- ¼ cup sugar
- 1 tsp. vanilla extract
- Topping: 12 oz. tub whipped topping

Instructions:
1. Coat cook pot with non-stick cooking spray.
2. Make cake batter according to box instructions.
3. Mix together egg, sugar, vanilla extract and cream cheese; combine until smooth.
4. Add cake batter into cook pot evenly.
5. Use a spoon and drop cream cheese mix by the spoonful, all over the cake batter.
6. Using a knife, drag through the cream cheese mixture to swirl through the cake batter.
7. Close lid and set to Slow Cooker LOW with a 3-hour timer, or cook on Slow Cooker HIGH for 1.5-2 hours. Test with a toothpick to determine if done. Toothpick will pull out clean when done.
8. Take lid off and remove cook pot once done. Let cake sit and cool completely.
9. Serve with whipped topping and enjoy.

Peach Dump Cake

Prep time: 15 minutes
Cook time: 2.5-3 hours
Yield: 8 servings

Ingredients:
- 16 oz. fresh or frozen peaches, sliced (undrained)
- 1 Tbsp. cornstarch
- ½ tsp. vanilla extract
- ¼ cup brown sugar
- ¼-½ tsp. cinnamon
- 1 box Jiffy white cake mix (or 1/2 package of a 2-layer size cake mix)
- 4 Tbsp. melted butter

Instructions:
1. Lightly grease the cook pot. Lay across the bottom.
2. Sprinkle peaches with cornstarch and toss lightly.
3. Drizzle with vanilla, then sprinkle the brown sugar over everything, and then the cinnamon.
4. Add the cake mix over the top of peach mixture. Drizzle the melted butter over cake mix as evenly as possible.
5. Close lid and set to Slow Cooker HIGH for 2.5-3 hours. If more time is needed, cook longer, using 15-minute increments.
6. Serve warm with vanilla ice cream or whipped topping. Enjoy!

Granny's Apple Delight

Prep time: 10 minutes
Cook time: 2 hours
Yield: 6-8 servings

Ingredients:

- 6 granny smith apples, peeled, cored and sliced
- 1 cup oatmeal
- 1 cup brown sugar
- 1/3 cup flour
- 1 tsp. cinnamon
- ¼ tsp. nutmeg
- 1 tsp. vanilla
- ½ cup butter or ½ cup margarine, melted
- Optional: ½ cup pecans

Instructions:

1. Mix sugar, flour, oatmeal, pecans and spices in a small bowl.
2. Stir vanilla and melted butter into mixture until it becomes crumbly.
3. Place half the sliced apples in the cook pot. Then, spoon half the oatmeal mix on top of the apples.
4. Repeat with the rest of the apples, then the rest of the oatmeal mixture.
5. Cover and set to Slow Cooker HIGH with a 2-hour timer. Check for doneness at 2 hours and add 30 minutes if necessary.
6. Best served hot with ice cream or drizzled with honey. Enjoy!

Pumpkin Caramel Cake

Prep time: 10 minutes
Cook time: 3 hours cook time
Yield: 8 servings

Ingredients:

- 1 box yellow cake mix
- 1 cup water
- 1/3 cup vegetable oil
- 3 eggs
- 1 (15 oz.) can pumpkin puree
- 1/3 cup brown sugar
- 1 tsp. cinnamon
- ¼ tsp. nutmeg
- ¼ tsp. ginger
- ¼ tsp. allspice
- 1 jar caramel topping
- Ice cream for serving

Instructions:

1. In a large mixing bowl, use a whisk to blend all ingredients together EXCEPT the caramel topping.
2. Spray the cook pot with non-stick cooking spray. Pour the batter into the cook pot.
3. Set the cooker to Slow Cook HIGH with a 2-hour timer. Cake will have begun to set, but should be a bit mushy on top.
4. Pour three quarters of the caramel sauce over the top of the cake.
5. Set to Slow Cooker HIGH and cook for 1 more hour. Check if cake is fully set, if not, cook for an additional 30 minutes or until set.
6. After cooking is complete, remove cook pot and set aside. Let cake cool for 10-15 minutes.
7. Best served warm with caramel drizzled over the top. Add a scoop of vanilla ice cream or whipped topping if preferred. Enjoy!

Lava Cake

Prep time: 15 minutes
Cook time: 2 hours
Yield: 8-10 servings

Ingredients:
- 1 boxed devils food cake
- 3 eggs
- 1/3 cup vegetable oil
- 1 2/3 cup water
- 1 pkg. Chocolate Instant Pudding Mix
- 2 cups cold milk
- 1 bag chocolate chips (sweet or semi-sweet)

Instructions:
1. Spray cook pot with non-stick cooking spray; set aside.
2. Mix cake mix, oil, eggs and water to a large bowl and mix well until combined.
3. Once mixed, pour batter into cook pot.
4. In medium bowl, whisk together the cold milk and pudding mix.
5. Once pudding has achieved a firm consistency, pour over cake batter in cook pot, but do not mix.
6. Sprinkle chocolate chips over top of pudding/cake.
7. Close lid and set to Slow Cooker HIGH with a 2-hour timer. Cake will be bubbly when finished.
8. Serve warm with a scoop of vanilla ice cream and enjoy.

Carrot Cake

Prep time: 10 minutes
Cook time: 1.5 hours
Yield: 8+ servings

Ingredients:
- 1 box carrot cake mix
- ½ cup applesauce
- 1 ⅓ cup water
- 3 eggs

Instructions:
1. Beat all ingredients together in stand mixer or in large bowl with hand mixer.
2. Spray inside of cook pot with non-stick cooking spray.
3. Pour batter into cook pot. Close lid.
4. Set cooker to Slow Cook HIGH and cook for 1.5 hours and check for doneness. If more time is needed, cook in 15-minute increments until done.
5. Once cake is finished, remove cook pot and let stand for 10-15 minutes to cool. Cut cake into pieces, frost individually and serve. Enjoy.

Lemon Pudding Cake

Prep time: 15 minutes
Cook time: 2 hours
Yield: 8+ servings

Ingredients:
- 3 large eggs, separated
- 1 tsp. lemon peel, grated
- ¼ cup lemon juice
- 3 Tbsp. butter
- 1 ½ cups milk
- ¾ cup sugar
- ¼ cup all-purpose flour
- 1/8 tsp. salt

Instructions:
1. Beat egg whites until stiff and peaks hold easily; set aside.
2. Next, beat the yolks, adding in the lemon juice, peel, milk and butter.
3. Mix flour, salt and sugar, then blend into the yolk mixture. Beat until smooth.
4. Gently fold into the egg whites.
5. Spoon into the cook pot. Close lid.
6. Set to Slow Cooker HIGH with a 2-hour timer.
7. Once complete, let cool for 10 minutes. Serve warm from cook pot. Enjoy!

Cherry Cheesecake Jubilee

Prep time: 30 minutes
Cook time: 2 hours
Yield: 8-10 servings

Ingredients:

Cheesecake Filling:
- 24 oz. cream cheese at room temperature
- 3 whole eggs
- ¾ cup granulated sugar
- 1½ tsp. pure vanilla extract
- 1 can cherry filling (for topping)

Graham Cracker Crust:
- 6 whole graham crackers crushed into crumbs
- 3 Tbsp. butter melted

Instructions:

Filling:
1. Using your stand mixer or a large bowl and hand mixer, mix cream cheese and sugar until combined well.
2. Add one egg at a time to the cream cheese mix, making sure to blend egg in well before adding the next egg. Once eggs are incorporated, mix in the vanilla extract. Set mixture to the side.

Crust:
1. In a medium bowl, mix butter and graham cracker crumbs using a fork. Blend until mixture looks like moist sand and clumps when squeezed.
2. Use a spring form pan that will fit inside cook pot. Press graham cracker crust into bottom of pan. Use the back of a spoon or measuring cup to press firm and flat, making sure entire bottom of pan is covered.
3. Add the cream cheese mixture over the crust using a spoon. Smooth over the crust forming an even layer.
4. Set the pan inside the cook pot. Using a spouted kettle or cup, carefully add up to 3 cups of water to cook pot. DO NOT get water into cheesecake pan. Stop adding water when the level has reached half way up cheesecake pan.
5. Close lid. Set cooker to Slow Cook HIGH with a 2-hour timer. Check the center of the cheesecake immediately with a thin knife. If cheesecake is still watery, cook for another 30 minutes, or until firm and no liquid is present in center.
6. Turn off cooker and let cheesecake cool for up to an hour. Lift the cake pan out and cover well with plastic or foil. Place in the fridge and let cool for another hour.
7. Serve with cherry topping and enjoy.

Seasonal and Party Beverages

Put your Multi-Cooker Express to the holiday test. Try some tasty party beverages that will please your guests. But, you don't need to reserve these recipes for parties. They are a great cold weather beverage, that will draw the family with great smells drifting throughout the house. I must admit, I have been known to enjoy a warm, comfort beverage on a rainy summer day as well.

Have fun with these and enjoy!

Hot Cocoa

Prep time: 5 minutes
Cook time: 1-2 hours
Yield: 6-8 serving

Ingredients:
- ½ cup baking cocoa
- 12 oz. can sweetened condensed milk
- 1/8 tsp. salt
- 7 ½ cups water
- 2 tsp. vanilla

Instructions:
1. In cook pot combine milk, water and vanilla.
2. Mix in cocoa and salt, blending until smooth.
3. Set to Slow Cook HIGH for 1 hour, or Slow Cook LOW for 2 hours.
4. Keep warm when finished and serve with mini marshmallows.

Pumpkin Spice Party Latte

Prep time: 10 minutes
Cook time: 1-2 hours
Yield: 6-8 servings

Ingredients:
- 6 cups strongly brewed coffee
- 5 cups 2% milk
- ½ cup pumpkin puree
- 1/3 cup vanilla extract
- ½ cup sugar
- 2 tsp. cinnamon
- 2 tsp. pumpkin pie spice

Instructions:
1. Pour coffee into cook pot. Add in milk and stir well.
2. In a medium bowl, mix together pumpkin puree, sugar, pumpkin pie spice, cinnamon and vanilla. Whip with whisk to combine.
3. Add pumpkin mixture to cook pot and mix well.
4. Turn on KEEP WARM setting and cover pot. Warm for 1-2 hours.
5. Serve and enjoy!

Spiced Vanilla Chai Latte

Prep time: 10 minutes
Cook time: 1.5 hours
Yield: 6-8 servings

Ingredients:

- 10 black tea bags-string removed
- 7 cups water
- 3 cups 2% or 1% milk
- ½ Tbsp. whole cloves
- 1½ tsp. ground cinnamon
- 10 thin slices of ginger root, (can substitute ½ tsp. ground ginger)
- ¾ tsp. nutmeg
- 1½ Tbsp. real vanilla extract
- ½ cup granulated sugar

Instructions:

1. Add the milk, water and tea bags to the cook pot. Stir well, careful not to tear bags.
2. Carefully stir in the rest of the ingredients.
3. Close lid. Set the cooker to Slow Cook HIGH with a 1.5-hour timer. Once done, use a strainer and strain into a serving container. Discard the solids.
4. Can be served hot are can be refrigerated and served cold. Can be stored in the fridge for 3-4 days. Use microwave to reheat.

Apple Cider

Prep time: 10 minutes
Cook time: 3 hours
Yield: Varies by portion size

Ingredients:
- 6-8 large apples, quartered
- 3-inch piece of fresh ginger, sliced thin
- 1 orange, quartered
- 4 cinnamon sticks
- 1-2 tsp. whole cloves
- Sweetener (sugar, maple syrup, honey or whatever you prefer)

Instructions:
1. Add the apples, cinnamon, orange, ginger and cloves to the cook pot.
2. Add water to the cook pot to the max fill line. Close lid.
3. Set the cooker to Slow Cook HIGH with a 3-hour timer. At 2 hours, open cooker and use a potato masher to mash the apples. Once done, cover and let cook cycle finish.
4. Once cider is done, pour through sieve to strain. Press solids to extract all liquid you can. Add cider back to cook pot.
5. Turn on the KEEP WARM setting and add in your sweetener of choice, blending well. Serve hot from cooker and enjoy.

Conclusion

Congratulations on reaching the end here. I hope you learned a lot about this remarkable cooker, and tried out all, if not most of the recipes. Remember, this is only the beginning, not the end.

Make sure to try all the recipes here, and alter them as you become more comfortable in both using this cooker and in your own culinary abilities. I have done my best here to provide as much variety of delicious recipes here for you to both try, and to cultivate the inner chef spirit within you. In addition, the recipes here cover the complete scope of the diverse ways on using the Crock Pot Express Multi Cooker, and you should now be familiar with all the different functionalities present in this kitchen appliance.

I want to personally thank you for taking the time to read my book, and hope it has provided value for you. I love hearing from my readers and how they feel about my work, so if you would be so kind, please log onto Amazon and leave a review for me and tell me what you thought! Was it better than you had anticipated? Was there a specific recipe you wished had been included? I am constantly improving and will listen to the feedback, in order to create a better edition of this book in the future. Thank you again, and god bless!

Sincerely,
Jason Koski

Printed in the USA
CPSIA information can be obtained
at www.ICGtesting.com
LVHW070152201123
764402LV00013B/410